8

MEGAWORDS

Multisyllabic Words for
Reading, Spelling, and Vocabulary

POLLY BAYRD · KRISTIN JOHNSON

Educators Publishing Service, Inc.

Cambridge and Toronto

Educators Publishing Service, Inc.

31 Smith Place, Cambridge, Massachusetts 02138-1089

Printed in U.S.A.
ISBN 0-8388-1840-4

Design by Persis Barron Levy

February 2002 Printing

CONTENTS

TO THE STUDENT

Megawords 8: Multisyllabic Words for Reading, Spelling, and Vocabulary is the last in a series of books designed to help you read and spell words that contain two or more syllables. The words are organized into lists according to their phonetic structure. Worksheets following each list explain and help you practice the rules or patterns found in that particular group of words. Some exercises focus on reading the words; others focus on spelling or vocabulary.

Megawords is designed to meet your individual learning needs. You and your teacher can decide which lists you need to study (and which you already know) by interpreting your results on the Check Test. You may need to focus on reading *and* spelling. Or you may need to use **Megawords** only to improve spelling skills. You and your teacher can record your progress on the Accuracy Checklist at the back of your book.

We think that it is important for you to be able to 1) sound out words and 2) learn to read them proficiently and fluently. You and your teacher will set a reading rate goal. When you can read the words easily and automatically, you will be less likely to forget the words and you can concentrate on reading for meaning instead of on sounding out words. You can keep track of your reading rate on the Proficiency Graph at the end of your book.

Megawords 8 focuses on assimilated prefixes. It assumes that you have mastered syllabication rules, common prefixes, suffixes, unaccented endings, and accent patterns. Many of the words in **Megawords 8** appeared in earlier lists in which the focus was on endings. Now you have an opportunity to review all of the skills you have previously studied. Because **Megawords 8** groups words according to prefixes, they have a variety of endings and accent patterns.

We hope that you will be interested in checking out your skills in reading and spelling multisyllabic words—in seeing what you know and what you need to learn. In addition, we hope that you will enjoy tackling new word groups and mastering them. We think that multisyllabic words, when presented clearly and in patterned groups, can be challenging and fun. We sincerely hope that you enjoy and experience success with **Megawords**.

Polly Bayrd
Kristin Johnson

LIST 39: ASSIMILATED PREFIX com-

com- (m)	com- (p)	com- (b)	cor- (r)	co- (vowels, some consonants)	con-
* command	* companion	* combination	* correct	* cooperate	* conductor
* comment	* compartment	* combine	* correction	* cooperation	* conference
* commerce	* compatible	combatant	* corrective	* coordinate	* confident
* commercial	* competition	combust	* correspond	coagulate	* confusion
* commission	* complain	combustion	* corrupt	coalesce	* congratulate
* commit	* complex		* corruption	coalition	* connect
* commitment	* complicated		correlate	coauthor	* connection
* committee	* comprehend	col- (l)	correlation	codefendant	* constitution
* commute	* compromise	* collect	correlative	coeducation	* continue
commander	* computer	* collection	correspondent	coerce	* contribute
commemorate	comparable	* college	corrigible	coercive	* convenient
commence	compassion	* collide	corroborate	coexist	* convince
commendatory	compel	collaborate	corrode	cogitate	conclude
commensurate	compensate	collapse	corrosion	cognition	conduct
commentary	compensatory	collate	corrosive	cohabit	confide
commiserate	competent	collateral	corrugate	coherent	congratulations
commissary	compile	colleague	corruptible	cohesive	connotation
commodious	complacent	collective		coincide	consecutive
commodity	complementary	collegiate		coincident	consequently
commotion	component	collision		convergent	considerable
	compose	colloquial		co-op	consideration
	composite			cooperative	consistency
	composure			coordination	contemplate
	comprehensive			coordinator	contingent
	compression			coworker	continuous
					conventional

*Practical spelling words. The teacher and student should decide together how many of these words the student will be responsible for spelling.

★ Sometimes the last letter of a prefix changes to match the first letter of the root that follows it. This makes words easier to pronounce. Such prefixes are called *assimilated prefixes.*

The prefix *com-* means "with" or "together," as in *commute* and *combine.*

com- changes to: *col-* before *l,* as in *collect*

              cor- before *r,* as in *corruption*

              co- before vowels, as in *cooperate*

              co- before other consonants, as in *cohesive*

              con- before other consonants, as in *confide*

com- is unchanged before *b, p,* and *m,* as in *combine, complain,* and *command.*

➤ Circle and pronounce the prefix *com-* in the following words. Then underline the letter that follows the prefix.

compatible	comparable	combatant	component	combine
combustion	compromise	competent	comprehend	compassion
competition				composure

★ The prefix *com-* is often followed by a root that begins with _____ or _____.

➤ Circle and pronounce the prefix *com-* or its assimilated prefix in each of the following words. Then underline the letter that follows each prefix.

commission	conference	coordinate	cooperate	collate
compel	corruptible	collateral	coordinator	commend
command	commercial	correct	collusion	confusion
correspond	continuous	corrode	commute	collision
coincide	collection	consecutive	coexist	compartment
correction	coalition	conductor	coworker	collateral
		commotion		

Review

Give an example for each rule.

com- changes to *co-* before vowels, as in _____.

com- changes to *cor-* before *r,* as in _____.

➡ Circle the prefix or assimilated prefix in these words. Underline the first letter of the root. Write the prefix and first letter of the root as shown. Then complete the rule.

(con)nection   __con__ + __n__   *com-* changes to _____ in front of _____,

conference   _____ + ____   ____, ____, ____, ____, ____, and some

conductor   _____ + ____   other consonants.

continue   _____ + ____

convince   _____ + ____

consequently   _____ + ____

commute   _____ + ____   *com-* doesn't change in front of _____, _____,

complain   _____ + ____   and _____.

combine   _____ + ____

collect   _____ + ____   *com-* changes to _____ in front of _____.

collision   _____ + ____

correct   _____ + ____   *com-* changes to _____ in front of _____.

corruption   _____ + ____

coalition   _____ + ____   *com-* changes to _____ in front of

cooperate   _____ + ____   _____.

coerce   _____ + ____

coincide   _____ + ____

➡ Your teacher will dictate some words that contain the prefix *com-*. Write the prefix or assimilated prefix and the first letter of the root as shown. Notice the double consonants in these words.

1. __com__ / __m__   3. _____ / ____   5. _____ / ____   7. _____ / ____

2. _____ / ____   4. _____ / ____   6. _____ / ____   8. _____ / ____

➡ Pronounce and combine the syllables. Then cover the divided word and practice reading the whole word. Study the accent pattern and draw a box around the accented syllable.

__ ´ __

com ment	comment
col lege	college
con duct	conduct

__ __ ´

com mand	command
col lapse	collapse
con duct	conduct

__ ´ __ __

con tem plate	contemplate
con fer ence	conference
com pro mise	compromise

__ __ ´ __

con tin gent	contingent
com part ment	compartment
col lec tion	collection

__ __ __ ´

co ex ist	coexist
co in cide	coincide
co a lesce	coalesce

__ __ ´ __ __

con grat u late	congratulate
con sis ten cy	consistency
con sec u tive	consecutive

__ __ __ ´ __

com pe ti tion	competition
cor re spon dent	correspondent
cor re la tion	correlation

__ ´ __ __ __

con se quent ly	consequently
com men tar y	commentary

__ __ __ __ ´ __

com mu ni ca tion	communication
con sid er a tion	consideration
con grat u la tions	congratulations
co or di na tion	coordination

__ __ __ ´ __ __

com ple men tar y	complementary
con sti tu tion al	constitutional

➡️ Match the prefixes with the roots to make words. Then say each word aloud as you write it.

con ——— erce _____   con   lide _____

com ——— lect _____   com   mend _____

col ——— rect _____   col   clude _____

cor ——— mand _____   cor   plain _____

co ——— vince _____convince_____   com   rode _____

➡️ Unscramble these multisyllabic words. If you circle the prefix and underline the suffix or a familiar ending, you will know which syllables begin and end the word.

lec (col) tive _____collective_____   cial mer com _____

con dence fi _____   mu cate ni com _____

ate op co er _____   spon cor dence re _____

tion tu sti con _____   ti pe com tion _____

Review

The prefix *com-* changes to *con-* before ____, ____, and some other consonants, *col-* before ____, *cor-* before ____, and *co-* before _____ and some other consonants.

➡️ Circle the first letter of the syllable next to the blank, and write the prefix *com-* or one of its assimilated prefixes in the blank. Use the review as a key. Then pronounce the word as you write it.

con (n)ect _____connect_____   ____ bi na tion _____

____ plex _____   ____ sis ten cy _____

____ ex ist _____   ____ re la tion _____

____ fi dent _____   ____ pro mise _____

____ mand _____   ____ in cide _____

____ lege _____   ____ lat er al _____

____ mit tee _____   ____ ven tion al _____

____ rec tion _____   ____ tin u ous _____

★ Many List 39 words have double consonants because the final letter of the prefix changes to match the first letter of the root. Remembering this will help you spell these words correctly.

➡ Fill in the blanks with one of the following combinations. Then write the whole word.

comm   coll   corr   **Copy**

1. To come together with force; to crash   _c_ _o_ _l_ _l_ ide   _collide_

2. To give an order to   — — — —and   _____

3. Evil; wicked   — — — —upt   _____

4. To travel regularly back and forth to work   — — — —ute   _____

5. To eat away gradually   — — — —ode   _____

6. To bring or gather together   — — — —ect   _____

7. To begin; to start   — — — —ence   _____

8. To fall in; to fold or shrink together   — — — —apse   _____

9. Business; buying and selling in large amounts   — — — —erce   _____

10. To arrange in order   — — — —ate   _____

11. To praise   — — — —   _____

12. A fellow worker   — — — —eague   _____

13. To exchange letters   — — — —e spond   _____

14. To express sympathy for   — — — —is er ate   _____

15. A pledge as security for a loan   — — — —at er al   _____

16. A group of people selected for a certain task   — — — —it tee   _____

17. To show the relationship between two things   — — — —e late   _____

➤ Your teacher will dictate some words. Sound out each word as you write the missing syllable(s). Then write the whole word, saying it aloud as you spell it. Remember that most words with assimilated prefixes have a double consonant.

Copy

1. _____ mence

2. _____ lapse

3. cor _____

4. _____ erce

5. _____ part _____

6. com _____ tee

7. _____ lec _____

8. cor _____ sion

9. _____ re _____ ent

10. _____ grat _____ late

11. _____ mit _____

12. col _____ sion

13. _____ pro _____

14. _____ a _____ tion

15. _____ tri _____

16. _____ pli _____ ed

➤ Unscramble the words below and spell them correctly in the blanks and circles. Both the words can be found in the list above.

MICEMETTO ○○ _ _ _ _ _ _ ○

COUNTATLARGE ○ _ _ _ ○ _ _ _ _ _ _ ○

➤ Unscramble the letters you have written in the circles to make another word from the list above:

_ _ _ _ _ _

➡ Identify the accented syllables. Then copy each word by syllables under the correct heading. Write the accented syllables in the boxes. Mark the accented vowels.

coerce	colleague	confident	continue	committee
conference	contingent	compromise	complicate	contribute
correlate	collegiate			

Accent the First Syllable   **Accent the Second Syllable**

cŏl	league

➡ Accent the root in the third syllable in words that have prefixes in both the first and second syllables.

comprehend	coincide	codefendant	coexist	correspondent
comprehension				coalesce

Accent the Third Syllable   **Accent the Third Syllable**

Separate and write the prefix (or assimilated prefix), root, and suffix in each of the following words. Then pronounce the words. Some words have more than one prefix or suffix.★

	Prefix	Root	Suffix	Double Letter?
conductor	con	duct	or	no
commission				
commitment				
corrective				
conference				
comparable				
coworker				
collective				
conventional				
compartment				
convenient				
consistently				
composite				
correspondent				
compatible				
incorrigible				
cohesive				
connection				
coincidence				
coexistent				

★In some words a consonant could be placed either at the end of the root or at the beginning of the suffix. As long as you can read and spell the word, it doesn't matter which way you divide it.

Accent patterns in words that have three or more syllables are often governed by a specific ending or an unaccented *i* or *u*. Accent the syllable just before syllables that contain *ti, ci,* or *si* (*-tion, -cial,* or *-sion*), unaccented *i* or *u*, and the *-ity* or *-ical* endings.

➡ Circle the final syllable (*-cial, -tion, -sion, -ity,* or *-ical*) or underline the unaccented *i* or *u*. Then copy the words by syllables, writing the accented syllables in the boxes. Mark long and short accented vowels and pronounce the words.

Three–Syllable Words

confusion   con   fū   sion

companion

connection

commission

Four–Syllable Words

commodity

coincidence

constitution

coalition

Five–Syllable Words

communicable

incorrigible

consideration

➡ Many List 39 words are hard to spell because the first syllable has a schwa sound. To spell these words correctly, write the prefix (or the assimilated prefix) in full and the root in full. Remember the double consonant in many of these words.

It sounds like . . .	but is spelled . . .
kə nect	* connect
kən duct	
kən fide	
kə mute	
kə mence	
kə man der	
kə mit	
kə mit tee	
kə mo tion	
kə rupt	
kə rode	
kə rec tion	*
kə rup tion	
kə lect	*
kə lapse	
kə lide	*
kə lec tion	*
kə lab or ate	
kə lec tive	

➡ Have another student test you on spelling the starred words. They are practical spelling words.

My score: _____ words correct.

Review

A word family is a group of words that have a common part. Adding various endings to the common part changes the part of speech or alters the meaning. For example, *memory, memorial, memorize,* and *memorandum* are members of the same word family. The common part is *memor*, which means "remember."

➤ Many words from List 39 belong to word families. They have the same prefix and root but different suffixes. In the blanks to the right of each word, write other words in the same word family. You may have to add, drop, or change some letters when you do this. Refer to List 39 and your dictionary. Some suffixes you might use are *-tion, -ive, -ate, -ed, -ing, -ous, -al, -able,* and *-tial*.

cooperate	_cooperation_	_cooperative_	_cooperating_
confide	_____	_____	_____
collect	_____	_____	_____
compare	_____	_____	_____
consider	_____	_____	_____
comprehend	_____	_____	_____
continue	_____	_____	_____

➤ Add suffixes to the following words. You may have to add, drop, or change some letters.

connect + tion	_____	coerce + ive	_____
consist + ent	_____	conduct + or	_____
consist + ency	_____	confuse + sion	_____
conclude + sion	_____	collide + sion	_____
coordinate + or	_____	college + ate	_____
coordinate + tion	_____	combust + ible	_____
commence + ment	_____	combust + tion	_____
convene + tion	_____	coincide + ent	_____
commerce + cial	_____	coincide + ence	_____

➡ Your teacher will dictate some practical spelling words. Say the words aloud as you write them under the correct heading.

con–

_____

_____

_____

_____

_____

com–

_____

_____

_____

_____

_____

col–

_____

_____

cor–

_____

_____

co–

_____

_____

Proofing Practice

➡ Two common List 39 words are misspelled in each of the sentences below. Correct them as shown.

commutes
1. My mom ~~comutes~~ by bus to the medical complecks.

2. The teacher asked Garrett to colect and korrect all the math papers.

3. The comitee was very confuzed by the proposed budget cuts.

4. I congratchulate you on your admission to colledge.

5. After the two school buses colided, the mayor set up a commishun to study driving practices.

➡ The Latin root *pos* means "to put" or "to place." When combined with the prefix *com-*, the resulting word suggests a "putting together." Fill in each blank with the correct word to complete the sentence.

compose   composers   composite   composition   composure

1. I was embarrassed, but I kept my _____. (1 Down)

2. What is the mineral _____ of this rock? (5 Across)

3. Have you ever tried to _____ a song? (5 Down)

4. Mozart and Bach were famous _____. (6 Across)

5. A finished jigsaw puzzle is a _____ of many pieces. (2 Down)

➡ The Latin root *mit* or *mis* means "to send." When combined with the prefix *com-*, the resulting word suggests a "sending together." Fill in each blank with the correct word to complete the sentence.

committed   commission   commitment   commissioner   committee

6. The criminally insane are _____ to mental hospitals. (3 Down)

7. The salespeople get a ten percent _____. (4 Across)

8. The mayor appointed a new police _____. (7 Across)

9. The planning _____ meets today at 4:00 P.M. (9 Across)

10. Rebecca made a _____ to live in Germany for one year. (8 Across)

→ Fill in each blank with a word from below that makes sense in the sentence. Use a dictionary to look up the meaning of unfamiliar words.

contingent	compatible	colloquial	consecutive	coagulate
commemorate	collaborated	collateral	coalition	convergent
commodious	complacently	coerced	commence	commiserate

1. When talking, we might use a _____ expression such as "I got an A on the exam," but when writing an essay we should say "I received an A on the examination."

2. The two friends got along well with each other. They were very _____.

3. The _____ lines came together in the center of the drawing.

4. The two factions of the political party formed a _____ to strengthen their position.

5. The author and the illustrator _____ to create a new children's book.

6. Roman emperors built arches to _____ their victories.

7. I always _____ with you about your misfortune but you never offer me support when I have problems.

8. I hope you were not _____ into signing that confession.

9. The winner of the chess match was smiling _____.

10. Our plans for a picnic are _____ on good weather. If it's sunny and warm, the picnic will start at noon.

11. Your blood will _____, or thicken, after you cut yourself. This prevents you from bleeding to death.

12. Ms. Alexander offered her car as _____ for a loan.

13. The dedication ceremony will _____, or begin, at two o'clock.

14. The _____ room was spacious enough to seat one hundred people.

15. This is the third _____ year that it has rained during our block party.

➡ Read the following sentences and circle all the List 39 words that you can find.

1. Ms. Edison is confident that a compromise will be reached.

2. The conference on computer skills will commence on Thursday.

3. It is more convenient for me to commute to work by bus than by car.

4. The principal will try to convince you to join the committee.

5. This computation is so complex, I don't think I'll get the correct answer.

6. The coordinator complained about the corrupt commissioner.

7. Open commentary and continuous cooperation are essential for coauthors.

8. You can find the combination lock in the glove compartment.

9. I commended my companion on his commitment to finish college.

10. Please continue to correspond with me about this complicated matter.

11. Mr. Hunter's commercial interests are not compatible with those of the food cooperative.

➡ Take out a piece of blank paper. Your teacher will dictate three of the sentences above for you to write.

➡ Now select ten words from List 39 and create a short story or a descriptive paragraph that uses those words. Be creative and avoid repetition!

Reading Accuracy: Demonstrate your accuracy in reading and spelling List 39 words. Your teacher will select ten words to read and ten practical spelling words for you to spell. Record your scores on the Accuracy Checklist. Work toward 90–100 percent accuracy.

Reading Proficiency: Now build up your reading fluency with List 39 words. Decide on your rate goal with your teacher. Record your progress on the Proficiency Graph.

My goal for reading List 39 is _____ words per minute with two or fewer errors.

LIST 40: ASSIMILATED PREFIX -ad

ad-, al- (l)	ac- (c), as- (s)	an- (n), af- (f), ag- (g)	ar- (r), at- (t)	ap- (p)
* addition	* accept	* affair	* arrest	* apparent
* address	* accomplish	* affect	* arrival	* appear
* adequate	* accuracy	* affection	* arrive	* appearance
* adjective	* accurate	* affectionate	* attain	* applaud
* administer	* assembly	* affirmative	* attempt	* appliance
* admire	* assert	* aggression	* attend	* application
* admission	* assertive	* aggressive	* attendance	* apply
* advertise	* assign	* announce	* attention	* appoint
* advice	* assignment	afferent	* attract	* appointment
* advise	* assist	affiliate	* attraction	* appreciate
* allegiance	* assistant	affinity	* attractive	* appropriate
* allow	* association	affirmation	array	* approval
* allowance	* assume	affix	arrears	* approve
addict	* assumption	affliction	arrogant	apparatus
additive	accelerate	affluent	attainable	apparition
adhesive	accent	aggravate	attentive	appeal
adjudicate	accessible	aggregation	attenuate	appendage
adjustment	accessories	annex	attest	appendicitis
adolescent	acclimated	annotate	attribute	appendix
adversity	accommodate	announcement	attrition	appreciation
advocate	accompany	annul		apprehend
allegation	accumulate			apprentice
alleviate	accuse			approach
alliteration	assessment			approximate
allocate	asset			approximation
allude	associate			
ally	assurance			

*Practical spelling words. The teacher and student should decide together how many of these words the student will be responsible for spelling.

Review

Sometimes the last letter of a prefix changes to match the first letter of the root that follows it. This makes words easier to pronounce. Such prefixes are called _____ prefixes.

★ The prefix *ad-* means "to" or "toward," as in *advice* and *addition*.

ad- changes to: *al-* before *l*, as in *alliance*

ac- before *c*, as in *accept*

as- before *s*, as in *assignment*

an- before *n*, as in *announce*

af- before *f*, as in *affect*

ag- before *g*, as in *aggression*

ar- before *r*, as in *arrange*

at- before *t*, as in *attempt*

ap- before *p*, as in *appear*

ad- is unchanged before other letters, as in *advice* and *administer*.

➡ Circle and pronounce the prefix *ad-* or its assimilated prefix in each of the following words. Then underline the letter that follows each prefix.

appliance	affirmative	assistant	allocate	adjudicate
annul	arrival	aggregation	affinity	accommodate
advertise	attempt	affectionate	assessment	accelerate
administer	affirmation	appendix	announce	arrest
accessible	additive	aggressive	attrition	associate
approximate	annotate	accumulate	alliteration	assembly
assignment		address		appreciate

Review

Give an example for each rule.

ad- changes to *ac-* before *c*, as in _____.

ad- changes to *ar-* before *r*, as in _____.

ad- changes to *at-* before *t*, as in _____.

ad- changes to *an-* before *n*, as in _____.

ad- is unchanged before other letters, as in _____.

➡ Circle the prefix or assimilated prefix in these words. Underline the first letter of the root. Write the prefix and first letter of the root as shown. Then complete the rule.

(ad)dress   __ad__ + __d__   *ad-* doesn't change in front of ____, ____, ____,

admission   ____ + ____   ____, ____, and some other letters.

adjective   ____ + ____

adolescent   ____ + ____

accept   ____ + ____   *ad-* changes to _____ in front of _____.

assign   ____ + ____   *ad-* changes to _____ in front of _____.

assembly   ____ + ____

announce   ____ + ____   _____ changes to _____ in front of ____.

affectionate   ____ + ____   _____ changes to _____ in front of ____.

aggressive   ____ + ____   _____ changes to _____ in front of ____.

aggravate   ____ + ____

allow   ____ + ____   _____ changes to _____ in front of ____.

arrest   ____ + ____   _____ changes to _____ in front of ____.

arrival   ____ + ____

attendance   ____ + ____   _____ changes to _____ in front of ____.

appear   ____ + ____   _____ changes to _____ in front of ____.

application   ____ + ____

➡ Your teacher will dictate some words that contain the prefix *ad-*. Write the prefix or assimilated prefix and the first letter of the root as shown. Notice the double consonants in these words.

1. __af__ / __f__   3. ____ / ____   5. ____ / ____   7. ____ / ____

2. ____ / ____   4. ____ / ____   6. ____ / ____   8. ____ / ____

➡ Match the prefixes with the roots to make words. Then say each word aloud as you write it.

as   low   _____   ar   gressive   _____

al   dict   _____   at   fair   _____

ad   sume   _____*assume*_____   ag   dress   _____

an   tend   _____   af   tempt   _____

at   nul   _____   ad   rest   _____

➡ Unscramble these multisyllabic words. If you circle the prefix and underline the suffix or a familiar ending, you will know which syllables begin and end the word.

trac at tion   _____   ga le al tion   _____

as ance sur   _____   ble ac si ces   _____

ant sist as   _____   ju ad cate di   _____

pri ate ap pro   _____   late mu cu ac   _____

as ci tion a so   _____

Review

The prefix *ad-* changes to *ac-* before _____, *af-* before _____, *as-* before _____, *ar-* before _____, *al-* before _____, *an-* before _____, *ag-* before _____, *ap-* before _____, and *at-* before _____.

➡ Circle the first letter of the syllable next to the blank, and write the prefix *ad-* or one of its assimilated prefixes in the blank. Use the review as a key. Then pronounce the word as you write it.

_____ fair   _____   _____ cur a cy   _____

_____ nex   _____   _____ o les cent   _____

_____ le giance   _____   _____ pli ca tion   _____

_____ sump tion   _____   _____ fec tion ate   _____

_____ ver si ty   _____   _____ ces so ries   _____

_____ low ance   _____   _____ pre ci ate   _____

_____ lo cate   _____   _____ pen di ci tis   _____

★ Many List 40 words have double consonants because the final letter of the prefix changes to match the first letter of the root. Remembering this will help you spell these words correctly.

➤ Fill in the blanks with one of the following combinations. Then write the whole word.

acc	aff	agg	all	ann	app	arr	ass	att

1. To give or appoint   __ __ __ign   _____

2. A person or nation united with
   another   __ __ __y   _____

3. To take or receive something   __ __ __ept   _____

4. To take to jail or court   __ __ __est   _____

5. Wealthy   __ __ __lu ent   _____

6. To add on   __ __ __ex   _____

7. To be present at   __ __ __end   _____

8. To reach the end of a journey   __ __ __ive   _____

9. To let or permit   __ __ __ow   _____

10. To draw toward someone or
    something   __ __ __ract   _____

11. To charge with having done
    something wrong   __ __ __use   _____

12. To name for an office or position   __ __ __oint   _____

13. Something having value   __ __ __et   _____

14. To express approval by clapping
    hands   __ __ __laud   _____

15. To make an effort at; to try   __ __ __empt   _____

16. To state positively; to declare   __ __ __ert   _____

17. Attacking; quarrelsome   __ __ __res sive   _____

18. To succeed in completing   __ __ __om plish   _____

Your teacher will dictate some words. Sound out each word as you write the missing syllable(s). Then write the whole word, saying it aloud as you spell it. Remember that most words with assimilated prefixes have a double consonant.

Copy

1. _____ vice   _____

2. _____ cuse   _____

3. af _____   _____

4. _____ no _____   _____

5. at _____ dance   _____

6. as _____ tant   _____

7. _____ low _____   _____

8. _____ gres _____   _____

9. _____ cur a _____   _____

10. ap _____ ance   _____

11. _____ ver _____   _____

12. _____ so _____ a _____   _____

13. _____ pli _____ tion   _____

14. _____ fec _____ate   _____

Find and circle the fourteen words you wrote above in the puzzle below. The words can be found in a straight line across or up and down.

```
A S S O C I A T I O N A F A P P E A R A N C E
N A F F E C T I O N A T E A H N A F E C T Y K
N D A T T E N D A N C E B I O T Z F A F R N J
O V C J P A P P L I C A T I O N U E L S P T B
T I A L O W A N C D U K Q V C A C C U R A C Y
A C E L R W D Y H A S S I S T A N T I O Q M G
T E A D V E R T I S E F M X A L L O W A N C E
E G A G G R E S S I O N S A P E A R E N C E E
```

Review

In two- and three-syllable words, accent the first syllable and pronounce the first vowel as if it were a short, long, *r*-controlled, or double-vowel sound in a one-syllable word. If that does not make a recognizable word, accent the second syllable, and pronounce the second vowel according to its syllabic type. This often gives the first vowel a schwa sound.

➡ Identify the accented syllables. Then copy each word by syllables under the correct heading. Write the accented syllables in the boxes. Mark the accented vowels.

additive	announcement	arrival	accurate	admission
aggravate	advertise	appearance	adequate	alliance
advocate	adhesive	accomplish	appliance	allocate

Accent the First Syllable   **Accent the Second Syllable**

Review

Match the rule with the word that is an example of that rule.

appearance   Accent the first syllable in most three-syllable words.

appreciation   Accent the root in most words with a prefix, root, and suffix.

additive   Accent the syllable just before *-tion* or *-sion*.

Separate and write the prefix (or assimilated prefix), root, and suffix in each of the following words. Then pronounce the words. One word has two suffixes.★

	Prefix	Root	Suffix	Double Letter?
accessible	_____	_____	_____	_____
advocate	_____	_____	_____	_____
assumption	_____	_____	_____	_____
announcement	_____	_____	_____	_____
affliction	_____	_____	_____	_____
adjustment	_____	_____	_____	_____
assessment	_____	_____	_____	_____
appearance	_____	_____	_____	_____
accurate	_____	_____	_____	_____
allocate	_____	_____	_____	_____
adjective	_____	_____	_____	_____
arrival	_____	_____	_____	_____
attendance	_____	_____	_____	_____
assignment	_____	_____	_____	_____
assistant	_____	_____	_____	_____
allowance	_____	_____	_____	_____
affectionate	_____	_____	_____ _____	_____
appointment	_____	_____	_____	_____
assertion	_____	_____	_____	_____

★In some words a consonant could be placed either at the end of the root or at the beginning of the suffix. As long as you can read and spell the word, it doesn't matter which way you divide it.

Review

Accent patterns in words that have three or more syllables are often governed by a specific ending or an unaccented *i* or *u*. Accent the syllable just before syllables that contain *ti, ci,* or *si* (-*tion, -cial,* or -*sion*), unaccented *i* or *u*, and the -*ity* or *ical* endings.

➡ Circle the final syllable (-*cial, -tion, -sion, -ity,* or -*ical*) or underline the unaccented *i* or *u*. Then copy the words by syllables, writing the accented syllables in the boxes. Mark long and short accented vowels and pronounce the words.

Three-Syllable Words

* allegiance _____ [ ] _____

attrition _____ [ ] _____

Four-Syllable Words

* appropriate _____ [ ] _____ _____

approximate _____ [ ] _____ _____

* appreciate _____ [ ] _____ _____

allegation _____ _____ [ ] _____

* application _____ _____ [ ] _____

Five-Syllable Words

appreciation _____ _____ _____ [ ] _____

* association _____ _____ _____ [ ] _____

approximation _____ _____ _____ [ ] _____

➡ Have another student test you on spelling the starred words. They are practical spelling words.

My score: _____ words correct.

A w_____ f_____ is a group of words that have a common part. Adding various endings to the common part changes the part of speech or alters the _____. For example, *memory, memorial, memorize,* and *memorandum* are members of the same word family. The common part is *memor,* which means "remember."

➡ Many words from List 40 belong to word families. They have the same prefix and root but different suffixes. In the blanks to the right of each word, write other words in the same word family. You may have to add, drop, or change some letters when you do this. Refer to List 40 and your dictionary. Some suffixes you might use are *-able, -ible, -ive, -tion, -sion, -or, -ed, -ing,* and *-ance.*

accept   _____   _____   _____

aggress   _____   _____   _____

accelerate   _____   _____   _____

apprehend   _____   _____   _____

appreciate   _____   _____   _____

add   _____   _____   _____

accumulate   _____   _____   _____

➡ Add suffixes to the following words. You may have to add, drop, or change some letters.

accuse + tion   _____   ally + ance   _____

access + ible   _____   affect + tion   _____

accompany + ist   _____   allow + ance   _____

accompany + ment   _____   allow + able   _____

assist + ant   _____   arrive + al   _____

assist + ance   _____   assess + or   _____

accurate + ly   _____   assert + ive   _____

accurate + cy   _____   assert + tion   _____

assess + ment   _____   attain + able   _____

apply + tion   _____   approve + al   _____

➡ Many List 40 words are hard to spell because the first syllable has a schwa sound. To spell these words correctly, write the prefix (or the assimilated prefix) in full and the root in full. Remember the double consonant in many of these words.

It sounds like . . .		but is spelled . . .
ə	dress	* _____
ə	di tion	* _____
ə	cuse	_____
ə	com mo date	_____
ə	sign	* _____
ə	sist ant	* _____
ə	nul	_____
ə	nounce	* _____
ə	fair	* _____
ə	fec tion ate	* _____
ə	rest	* _____
ə	ri val	* _____
ə	tempt	* _____
ə	ten dance	* _____
ə	pear	* _____
ə	prove	* _____
ə	point ment	* _____
ə	pre ci ate	* _____

➡ Have another student test you on spelling the starred words. They are practical spelling words.

My score: _____ words correct.

➡ Your teacher will dictate some practical spelling words. Say the words aloud as you write them under the correct heading.

ad–

_____

_____

an–

_____

_____

ar–

_____

ac–

_____

ap–

_____

_____

_____

at–

_____

_____

as–

_____

_____

ag–

_____

af–

_____

al–

_____

Proofing Practice

➡ Two common List 40 words are misspelled in each of the sentences below. Correct them as shown.

1. The police ~~attemted~~ *attempted* to arest the burglar.

2. Some famous people do not appreceate undue atenshun from reporters.

3. Ellie is an afeksionate and attracktive child.

4. Apointment of cabinet members is subject to approvel by Congress.

5. The shop assistent earned a weekly alowence.

➡ When the Latin root *pare* or *pear* is combined with the assimilated prefix *ap-*, it means "to show to" someone. Fill in each blank with the correct word to complete the sentence.

appeared	apparent	apparitions	appearance	apparently

1. It was the singer's first _____ in this city.

2. She was _____ on a nationwide tour.

3. The audience's reception made it _____ that she was quite popular.

4. When she _____ on stage, the crowd applauded and cheered.

5. In *A Christmas Carol,* Scrooge sees three ghosts, or _____ .

➡ When the Latin root *plic* is combined with the assimilated prefix *ap-*, it means "to attach to." Fill in each blank with the correct word to complete the sentence.

applied	applicable	appliances	application	applicants

6. Mr. Sherman filled out an _____ for the job.

7. He was one of many _____ for the job.

8. Because of his experience, he had many _____ skills.

9. He was adept at repairing small _____ such as toasters.

10. Unfortunately, many other well-qualified people also _____ for the job.

➡ When the Latin root *tend* is combined with the assimilated prefix *at-*, it means "to stretch toward."

attend	attention	attendant	attendance	attentive

11. Children must _____ school.

12. The teacher checks their _____ daily.

13. Those children were very _____ as they listened to the story.

14. A bell called the teacher's _____ to the time.

15. The playground _____ watched the children during recess.

→ Fill in each blank with a word from below that makes sense in the sentence. Use a dictionary to look up the meaning of unfamiliar words.

attrition	alliteration	ally	arrogant	allocated
affluent	affinity	allegation	adjudicate	affirmative
adversities	affiliated	acclimated	alleviate	attenuate

1. Although the boys' school and the girls' school did not have the same staff, they were

   _____ .

2. We knew his answer would be in the _____ when we saw him
   nodding his head and smiling.

3. There are many _____ families in this oil-rich part of Texas.

4. The judge will _____ this case next week.

5. A series of _____ had left the family homeless.

6. When we moved to Alaska, it took me awhile to get _____ to
   the cold winters.

7. Cecilia is naturally attracted to outside sports. She has an _____
   for skiing, hiking, and hang gliding.

8. The aspirin will help _____ your pain.

9. The repetition of the /s/ sound in "the sun sank slowly" is an example of

   _____ .

10. The foundation _____ large sums of money to the children's
    hospital.

11. Great Britain was an _____ of the United States in World War II.

12. Famine could severely _____ the population of some third-world
    countries.

13. The employer hoped that enough people would leave through _____
    so that she would not have to dismiss anyone.

14. The doctor's _____ attitude caused people to dislike him.

15. The lawyer's _____ was proved when the surprise witness took
    the stand.

➡ Read the following sentences and circle all the List 40 words that you can find.

1. Your aggressive and arrogant behavior accomplishes nothing.

2. When he had appendicitis, Assad was accompanied to the hospital by an associate.

3. The assistant nurse was attentive to the patients.

4. When I arrive, I will assist the accountant.

5. Margaret was assertive, though not aggressive, in her attempt to provide better than adequate service.

6. Byron will get more money for his allowance if he completes his assignments.

7. Ms. Dominic appreciates trainees who have a positive attitude.

8. If you can afford to advertise, more people will apply for the job.

9. The accountant announced that the cooperative should seek out financial advice.

10. The appearance of the president attracted a great deal of attention.

➡ Take out a piece of blank paper. Your teacher will dictate three of the sentences above for you to write.

➡ Now select ten words from List 40 and create a short story or a descriptive paragraph that uses those words. Be creative and avoid repetition!

Reading Accuracy: Demonstrate your accuracy in reading and spelling List 40 words. Your teacher will select ten words to read and ten practical spelling words for you to spell. Record your scores on the Accuracy Checklist. Work toward 90–100 percent accuracy.

Reading Proficiency: Now build up your reading fluency with List 40 words. Decide on your rate goal with your teacher. Record your progress on the Proficiency Graph.

My goal for reading List 40 is _____ words per minute with two or fewer errors.

LIST 41: ASSIMILATED PREFIX sub-

sub-	sub-	suc- (c), suf- (f)	sup- (p), sug- (g)	sus- (c, p, t), sur- (r)
* subject	subservient	* succeed	* suggest	* suspect
* submarine	subside	* success	* suggested	* suspicious
* submit	subsidiary	* successful	* suggestion	surreptitious
* subscribe	subsidize	* suffer	* supplies	surrogate
* subscription	subsidy	* sufficient	* supply	susceptibility
* substitute	subsist	succession	* support	susceptible
* subtract	subsistence	successive	* suppose	suspend
* subtraction	substance	successor	suggestibility	suspender
* suburb	substandard	succinct	suggestible	suspense
* suburban	substantial	succor	suggestive	suspension
subconscious	substantiate	succumb	supplant	suspicion
subcontract	substantive	sufferable	supple	sustain
subculture	substitution	sufferance	supplement	sustenance
subdivide	substratum	suffice	supplementary	
subdue	substructure	suffix	supplicate	
subjection	subtotal	suffocate	supportive	
subjugate	suburbanite	suffrage	supposition	
sublease	subversion	suffragist	suppository	
sublimate	subversive	suffuse	suppress	
submerge			suppression	
submission			suppressive	
subordinate				
subpoena				
subsequent				

*Practical spelling words. The teacher and student should decide together how many of these words the student will be responsible for spelling.

★ The prefix *sub-* means "under" or "below," as in *subject* and *submarine*.

sub- changes to: *suc-* before *c*, as in *success*

suf- before *f,* as in *suffer*

sup- before *p*, as in *suppose*

sug- before *g*, as in *suggest*

sur- before *r,* as in *surrogate*

sus- before *p* and *t,* as in *suspend* and *sustain*

sub- is unchanged before other letters, as in *submarine*.

➡ Circle and pronounce the prefix *sub-* or its assimilated prefix in each of the following words. Then underline the letter that follows each prefix.

subjection	succession	substitute	surrogate	suggestibility
subscription	suspend	suburban	suffer	sustain
succor	sustenance	suffering	suggest	suspension
successful	subscribe	suffocate	suffix	suspicion

➡ Find and circle the twenty words above in the puzzle below. The words can be found in a straight line across or up and down. Write the leftover letters in the blanks below.

```
S U G G E S T I B I L I T Y S U C C O R O
U S U B J E C T I O N U T S U F F I X S S
C S S U S T E N A N C E I D C E S H S U U
C S O S W I S A P S U F F O C A T E U B B
E U S U S T A I N O S U F F E R I N G U S
S S O F R S U B S U S P E N S I O N G R C
S P S F T S U S P I C I O N S I T U E B R
I E T E E S U R R O G A T E F F O R S A I
O N I R N N E S U B S T I T U T E R T N B
N D S U B S C R I P T I O N L W O R T H E
```

_____ ____ __ _ _____

_____ ___ _____ _____. —AESOP

33

➡ Circle the prefix or assimilated prefix in these words. Underline the first letter of the root. Write the prefix and first letter of the root as shown. Then complete the rule.

(sub)stitute   _**sub**_ + _**s**_   *sub-* doesn't change in front of _____, _____,

subjection   _____ + _____   _____, the v_ _ _ _s and some other letters.

subversive   _____ + _____

suburban   _____ + _____

subordinate   _____ + _____

success   _____ + _____   *sub-* changes to _____ in front of _____.

succumb   _____ + _____

suffer   _____ + _____   *sub-* changes to _____ in front of _____.

sufficient   _____ + _____

support   _____ + _____   _____ changes to _____ in front of

suppression   _____ + _____   _____.

suggest   _____ + _____   _____ changes to _____ in front of

suggestion   _____ + _____   _____.

sustain   _____ + _____   _____ changes to _____ in front of

suspend   _____ + _____   _____ and _____.

surrogate   _____ + _____   _____ changes to _____ in front of

surreptitious   _____ + _____   _____.

➡ Your teacher will dictate some words that contain the prefix *sub-*. Write the prefix or assimilated prefix and the first letter of the root as shown. Notice the double consonants in these words.

1. _**suf**_ / _**f**_   3. _____ /_____   5. _____ /_____   7. _____ /_____

2. _____ /_____   4. _____ /_____   6. _____ /_____   8. _____ /_____

➡ Match the prefixes with the roots to make words. Then say each word aloud as you write it.

suc	fix	_____	sup	cinct	_____
sus	ply	_____	sub	pose	_____
sup	lease	_____	suc	gest	_____
sub	cess	*success*	suf	tract	_____
suf	pect	_____	sug	fer	_____

➡ Unscramble these multisyllabic words. If you circle the prefix and underline the suffix or a familiar ending, you will know which syllables begin and end the word.

cious cons sub	_____		pen sus der	_____	
quent se sub	_____		suf cient fi	_____	
tive sup por	_____		jec sub tive	_____	
ges tion sug	_____		pi sus cion	_____	

Review

The prefix *sub-* changes to *suc-* before _____, *suf-* before _____, *sup-* before _____, *sug-* before _____, *sur-* before _____, and *sus-* before _____, _____ , and _____.

➡ Circle the first letter of the syllable next to the blank, and write the prefix *sub-* or one of its assimilated prefixes in the blank. Use the review as a key. Then pronounce the word as you write it.

_____ plant	_____	_____ fix	_____
_____ ju gate	_____	_____ ces sor	_____
_____ pres sion	_____	_____ ges ti ble	_____
_____ pos i tor y	_____	_____ rep ti tious	_____
_____ stan ti ate	_____	_____ or di nate	_____
_____ sid i ar y	_____	_____ sti tu tion	_____

★ Many List 41 words have double consonants because the final letter of the prefix changes to match the first letter of the root. Remembering this will help you spell these words correctly.

➡ Fill in the blanks with one of the following combinations. Then write the whole word.

succ	suff	supp	sugg	surr

Copy

1. To keep from failing; to hold up   — — — —ort   _____

2. Opposite of *prefix*   — — — —ix   _____

3. Expressed briefly and clearly   — — — —inct   _____

4. To assume; to consider as possible   — — — —ose   _____

5. To have pain or grief   — — — —er   _____

6. To put an end to; to stop by force   — — — —ress   _____

7. A favorable result; good fortune   — — — —ess   _____

8. Bending easily   — — — —le   _____

9. To bring to mind; to propose   — — — —est   _____

10. To furnish; to provide   — — — —ly   _____

11. To be enough; to satisfy   — — — —ice   _____

12. Something added; to supply what

    is lacking   — — — —le ment   _____

13. Enough   — — — —i cient   _____

14. To smother; to stifle   — — — —o cate   _____

15. A substitute   — — — —o gate   _____

Review

Give an example for each rule.

sub- changes to *suf-* before *f*, as in _____ .

sub- changes to *sup-* before *p*, as in _____ .

sub- changes to *sur-* before *r*, as in _____ .

Your teacher will dictate some words. Sound out each word as you write the missing syllable(s). Then write the whole word, saying it aloud as you spell it.

Copy

1. _____ urb   _____

2. suf _____   _____

3. _____ press   _____

4. _____ pense   _____

5. sub _____   _____

6. _____ ges _____   _____

7. sub _____ sion   _____

8. _____ ro _____   _____

9. sus _____ cious   _____

10. _____ ma _____   _____

11. _____ fo _____   _____

12. sub _____ tial   _____

13. sug _____ i ble   _____

14. _____ cons _____   _____

15. _____ po _____ tion   _____

16. _____ sti _____   _____

Unscramble the words below and spell them correctly in the blanks and circles. Both words can be found in the list above.

USISNOVERB   _ ◯ ◯ _ _ _ ◯ _ _ _

STARTCUB   _ ◯ ◯ _ ◯ _ _ _

Unscramble the letters you have written in the circles to make another word from the list above:

_ _ _ _ _ _

In two- and three-syllable words, accent the first syllable and pronounce the first vowel as if it were a short, long, *r*-controlled, or double-vowel sound in a one-syllable word. If that does not make a recognizable word, accent the second syllable, and pronounce the second vowel according to its syllabic type.

➤ Identify the accented syllables. Then copy each word by syllables under the correct heading. Write the accented syllables in the boxes. Mark the accented vowels.

substantive	successive	suggestion	sublimate	substitute
subsequent	suburban	supportive	suffocate	subculture
subscription		subsistence		substandard

Accent the First Syllable   **Accent the Second Syllable**

➤ Notice how the accent pattern changes in words as they become longer.

sustain

substitute

substance

sustenance

substitution

substantiate

➤ Separate and write the prefix (or assimilated prefix), root, and suffix in each of the following words.★ Then pronounce the words.

	Prefix	Root	Suffix	Double Letter?
subsidize	_____	_____	_____	_____
sufferance	_____	_____	_____	_____
subjection	_____	_____	_____	_____
sustenance	_____	_____	_____	_____
substantial	_____	_____	_____	_____
subsistence	_____	_____	_____	_____
subscription	_____	_____	_____	_____
succession	_____	_____	_____	_____
successful	_____	_____	_____	_____
suggestion	_____	_____	_____	_____
suppressive	_____	_____	_____	_____
suspension	_____	_____	_____	_____
supportive	_____	_____	_____	_____
suggestible	_____	_____	_____	_____
successor	_____	_____	_____	_____
substandard	_____	_____	_____	_____
subtraction	_____	_____	_____	_____

Review

Match each word with its accent pattern.

__ __ ´__ __ __   subsidiary   __ __ __ ´__   suggestible

__ __ __ ´__ __   supplementary   __ __ ´__ __   substitution

★In some words a consonant could be placed either at the end of the root or at the beginning of the suffix. As long as you can read and spell the word, it doesn't matter which way you divide it.

Review

Accent patterns in words that have three or more syllables are often governed by a specific ending or an unaccented *i* or *u*. Accent the syllable just before syllables that contain *ti, ci,* or *si* (*-tion, -cial,* or *-sion*), unaccented *i* or *u*, and the *-ity* or *-ical* endings.

➤ Circle the final syllable (*-tial, -tion, -sion, -ity,* or *-ical*) or underline the unaccented *i* or *u*. Then copy the words by syllables, writing the accented syllables in the boxes. Mark long and short accented vowels and pronounce the words.

Three-Syllable Words

sublime   ☐ ____ ____

substantial   ____ ☐ ____

subversion   ____ ☐ ____

suspicious   ____ ☐ ____

subconscious   ____ ☐ ____

sufficient   ____ ☐ ____

Four-Syllable Words

subservient   ____ ☐ ____ ____

substitution   ____ ____ ☐ ____

susceptible   ____ ☐ ____ ____

substantiate   ____ ☐ ____ ____

surreptitious   ____ ____ ☐ ____

subordinate   ____ ☐ ____ ____

Five-Syllable Words

subsidiary   ____ ☐ ____ ____ ____

suppository   ____ ☐ ____ ____ ____

Six-Syllable Words

suggestibility   ____ ____ ′ ____ ☐ ____ ____

susceptibility   ____ ____ ′ ____ ☐ ____ ____

Review

A w_____ f_____ is a group of words that have a common part. Adding various endings to the common part changes the part of speech or alters the _____. For example, *memory, memorial, memorize,* and *memorandum* are members of the same word family. The common part is *memor,* which means "remember."

➤ Many words from List 41 belong to word families. They have the same prefix and root but different suffixes. In the blanks to the right of each word, write other words in the same word family. You may have to add, drop, or change some letters when you do this. Refer to List 41 and your dictionary. Some suffixes you might use are *-tial, -ive, -ful, -ing, -ed, -ible, -tion, -sion, -or,* and *-ate.*

substance   _____   _____   _____

success   _____   _____   _____

suffer   _____   _____   _____

suggest   _____   _____   _____

subscribe   _____   _____   _____

➤ Add suffixes to the following words. You may have to add, drop, or change some letters.

subject + tion	_____	submit + sion	_____
subject + ed	_____	submit + ive	_____
subsist + ence	_____	subsidy + ize	_____
suburb + an	_____	substitute + tion	_____
subscribe + tion	_____	subside + ary	_____
suffice + ent	_____	support + ive	_____
suffice + ency	_____	supplement + ary	_____
suspend + sion	_____	suppress + sion	_____
suspend + er	_____	suppress + ive	_____
sustain + ance	_____	supply + es	_____
subvert + sion	_____	subdivide + sion	_____
suffrage + ist	_____	suppose + ed	_____

➡ Your teacher will dictate some practical spelling words. Say the words aloud as you write them under the correct heading.

sub-

_____

_____

_____

_____

sup-

_____

_____

_____

sus-

_____

suc-

_____

_____

suf-

_____

sug-

_____

_____

Proofing Practice

➡ Two common List 41 words are misspelled in each of the sentences below. Correct them as shown.

     substitute
1. The butter ~~substatute~~ was not very sucessful in the taste tests.

2. The crew in World War I submareens often lacked suplies of fresh fruit and vegetables.

3. The salesperson sugested that I subskribe to the magazine.

4. That child is behaving in a suspiscious manner; do you supose she is the one who took

   the cookies?

5. Are your skills in addition and subtracktion suficient for calculating the subtotal?

➡ Read each group of words below. Then fill in each blank with a word that makes sense in the sentence.

suggest   suggestibility   suggestion   suggestive   suggested

suggestible

1. I'd like to _____ that we go swimming this afternoon.

2. Tracy, however, had another _____.

3. She _____ that we go to the zoo.

4. Martin could be talked into anything. He was _____.

5. In fact, Martin's _____ was apparent when Dolores suggested sky

   diving.

6. Dolores had many ideas. She came up with a _____ list of activities.

suffers   insufferable   suffragist   suffering   suffrage

7. John _____ from migraine headaches.

8. Television has made us more aware of the _____ in drought-stricken

   Africa.

9. The United States granted _____ to women in 1920.

10. Sometimes I feel that the pain from a dentist's drill is _____.

11. Susan B. Anthony was a famous _____.

success   successive   succession   successful   successor

12. It rained for three _____ days.

13. The party was a great _____.

14. Mr. Palmer is a _____ business school graduate.

15. Bill Clinton was George Bush's _____ as president of the United

   States.

16. Prince Charles is next in the line of _____ to the British throne.

➡ Fill in each blank with a word from below that makes sense in the sentence. Use a dictionary to look up the meaning of unfamiliar words. Then complete the puzzle.

supplementary	subservient	supplanted	subsidiary	subsidy
surreptitious	supplicated	surrogate	succor	subjugated

Across

1. The criminal _____ the judge for a shorter sentence.

3. The fugitive behaved in a _____ manner.

5. Charlemagne _____ the Saxons after a long struggle in the eighth

  century.

6. The relief workers offered aid and _____ to the victims of the flood.

7. The baseball coach expects his players to be _____ and do as he says.

8. Machinery has _____ hand labor in making shoes.

9. The baby had some milk but needs a _____ feeding of cereal.

Down

1. The _____ mother gave birth to a healthy baby.

2. The bus line is a _____ of the railroad. It is owned by another company.

4. The student received a _____ from the government for education.

➡ Read the following sentences and circle all the List 41 words that you can find.

1. If you want to succeed, you will have to make a sustained effort.

2. The substitute teacher suggested that the students practice the subtraction facts.

3. Suffice it to say that your suspicions should be kept to yourself.

4. I suppose my subscription to this magazine needs to be renewed.

5. Submit your request for more supplies to my successor.

6. Do suburban libraries receive substantial support from patrons?

7. The successful lawyer was supportive of the new tax laws.

8. Many people suffer from insufficient health care.

9. The only suspect looks very suspicious.

10. Ms. Oliver supplements her income by selling newspaper subscriptions.

11. The submarine was involved in subversive activities.

➡ Take out a piece of blank paper. Your teacher will dictate three of the sentences above for you to write.

➡ Now select ten words from List 41 and create a short story or a descriptive paragraph that uses those words. Be creative and avoid repetition!

Reading Accuracy: Demonstrate your accuracy in reading and spelling List 41 words. Your teacher will select ten words to read and ten practical spelling words for you to spell. Record your scores on the Accuracy Checklist. Work toward 90–100 percent accuracy.

Reading Proficiency: Now build up your reading fluency with List 41 words. Decide on your rate goal with your teacher. Record your progress on the Proficiency Graph.

My goal for reading List 41 is _____ words per minute with two or fewer errors.

LIST 42: ASSIMILATED PREFIXES *ob-* AND *dis-*

ob-, *op- (p)*	*oc- (c)*, *of- (f)*	*dis-*	*dis-*	*dif- (f)*	*di- (m, v, l, g)*
* object	* occasion	* disagree	dismiss	* difference	* divide
* objection	* occasionally	* disappear	dismissal	* different	* division
* observe	* occupation	* disapprove	disorganize	* difficult	digest
* opponent	* occurrence	* discount	displeasure	* difficulty	digestion
* opposite	* offer	* discover	dispose	differ	digestive
obedient	occlude	* disease	disposition	differential	digress
obese	occult	* disobey	disqualify	differentiate	dilapidated
objectionable	occupant	* disturb	disservice	diffident	dilate
objective	occupy	disability	dissolve	diffuse	dilute
obligation	occur	disabled	distemper	diffusion	dimension
oblige	occurred	disadvantage	distinguished		dimensional
obnoxious	offend	disagreement	distribute		diminish
obscure	offense	disappoint	disturbance		diverge
observation	offensive	disarray			diversion
obsolete	offering	disaster			divert
obstacle		disclose			divulge
obstinate		discontented			
obstruction		discontinue			
obtain		discriminate			
obvious		discussion			
opportunity		disgraceful			
oppose		disguise			
opposition		dishonest			
oppress		disinfect			
oppression		dislocate			
oppressive		dismantle			

*Practical spelling words. The teacher and astudent should decide together how many of these words the student will be responsible for spelling.

46

Review

_____ _____ are prefixes in which the last letter of the prefix changes to match or better fit with the first letter of the root that follows it.

★ The prefix *ob-* means "in the way" or "against," as in *obstacle* and *object*.

ob- changes to: *op-* before *p*, as in *oppose*

oc- before *c*, as in *occupy*

of- before *f*, as in *offer*

ob- is unchanged before other letters, as in *observe* and *object*.

➡ Circle and pronounce the prefix *ob-* or its assimilated prefix in the following words. Then underline the letter that follows each prefix.

occur	offend	occupation	opposite	observe
offering	obstruction	opposition	opponent	occasional
obnoxious	occasion	obvious	object	opportunity
obstinate	oppose	obligation	obscure	oppress
obtain	obedient	offensive	occult	occurrence

★ The prefix *dis-* means "not," "opposite of," or "deprive of."

dis- changes to: *dif-* before *f*, as in *differ*

di- before *l, v, m,* and *g* (sometimes), as in *diversion, diminish,* and *digest*

dis- is unchanged before vowels and most other consonants, as in *disagree, disobey, disturb,* and *dispose*.

➡ Circle and pronounce the prefix *dis-* or its assimilated prefix in the following words. Then underline the letter that follows each prefix.

disobey	disinfect	digest	diminish	disagree
difference	disease	digress	diffusion	disguise
divide	discover	disturb	disabled	digestion
diverge	division	disaster	dissolve	dispose
dismiss	difficult	diffuse	discount	dimension

➡ Circle the prefix or assimilated prefix in these words. Underline the first letter of the root. Write the prefix and first letter of the root as shown. Then complete the rule.

(ob)jection	__ob__ + __j__	ob- doesn't change in front of ____, ____, ____,
observe	_____ + ____	____, and some other letters.
obvious	_____ + ____	
obligation	_____ + ____	
offend	_____ + ____	ob- changes to _____ in front of ____.
offer	_____ + ____	
opponent	_____ + ____	ob- changes to _____ in front of ____.
occupy	_____ + ____	ob- changes to _____ in front of ____.
disappear	_____ + ____	dis- doesn't change in front of v_____s and
disobey	_____ + ____	most c_____s.
disinfect	_____ + ____	
disclose	_____ + ____	
dismiss	_____ + ____	
difference	_____ + ____	dis- changes to _____ in front of ____.
diversion	_____ + ____	dis- sometimes changes to _____ in front of
dilate	_____ + ____	____, ____, ____, and ____.
diminish	_____ + ____	
digest	_____ + ____	

➡ Your teacher will dictate some words that contain the prefixes *dis-* and *ob-*. Write the assimilated prefix and the first letter of the root as shown. Notice the double consonants in these words.

1. __oc__ / __c__   3. _____ / ____   5. _____ / ____   7. _____ / ____

2. _____ / ____   4. _____ / ____   6. _____ / ____   8. _____ / ____

Pronounce and combine the syllables. Then cover the divided word and practice reading the whole word. Study the accent patterns and draw a box around the accented syllables.

__ ´__

of fer	offer
dif fer	differ

__ __´

ob tain	obtain
dis turb	disturb

__ ´__ __

dif fer ence	difference
ob sta cle	obstacle

__ __´__

ob jec tion	objection
dis cov er	discover

__ __ __´

dis ap point	disappoint
dis ap prove	disapprove

__ ´__ __ __

dif fi cul ty	difficulty

__ __ __´__

op po si tion	opposition
ob ser va tion	observation
dis con tin ue	discontinue
dif fer en tial	differential

__ __´__ __

dis crim i nate	discriminate
dis qual i fy	disqualify

__ __ __´__ __

op por tu ni ty	opportunity
ob jec tiv i ty	objectivity
dif fer en ti ate	differentiate

__ __´__ __ __

di lap i da ted	dilapidated
oc ca sion al ly	occasionally

__ __ __ __´__ __

dis crim i na tion	discrimination

➡ Match the prefixes with the roots to make words. Then say each word aloud as you write it.

oc	fer	_____	op	pose	_____
dif	count	_____	di	tain	_____
ob	cur	*occur*	of	fend	_____
dis	ject	_____	ob	gest	_____
of	scure	_____	dis	fense	_____
ob	fer	_____	of	lute	_____
di	turb	_____	oc	pose	_____
dis	late	_____	di	cur	_____

➡ Unscramble these multisyllabic words. If you circle the prefix and underline the suffix or a familiar ending, you will know which syllables begin and end the word.

tion jec ob	_____		ive ob ject	_____	
miss al dis	_____		rence cur oc	_____	
dif ent fer	_____		sion di men	_____	
ing fer of	_____		fen of sive	_____	

po dis si tion   _____

al oc ca sion   _____

ob tion ser va   _____

cu oc pa tion   _____

Review

Give an example for each rule.

ob- changes to *op-* before *p*, as in _____.

ob- changes to *oc-* before *c*, as in _____.

ob- changes to *of-* before *f*, as in _____.

Review

The prefix *ob-* changes to *oc-* before _____, to *of-* before _____, and to *op-* before _____.

The prefix *dis-* changes to *dif-* before _____ and to _____ before *g, v, l,* and *m* (sometimes).

➤ Circle the first letter of the root and write *ob-*, *dis-*, or one of their assimilated prefixes in the blank. Use the review as a key. Then pronounce the word as you write it.

Add *ob-*, *oc-*, *of-*, or *op-*	**Copy**	**ABC Order**
_____ vi ous	_____	_____
_____ cur	_____	_____
_____ fer ing	_____	_____
_____ po site	_____	_____
_____ fen sive	_____	_____
_____ tain	_____	_____
_____ cu py	_____	_____
_____ press	_____	_____
_____ ject	_____	_____

Add *dis-*, *dif-*, or *di–*	**Copy**	**ABC Order**
_____ fer	_____	_____
_____ count	_____	_____
_____ miss al	_____	_____
_____ hon est	_____	_____
_____ close	_____	_____
_____ fi cult	_____	_____
_____ late	_____	_____
_____ gest	_____	_____
_____ men sion	_____	_____

➤ Now go back and write the words in alphabetical order.

★ Many List 42 words have double consonants because the final letter of the prefix changes to match the first letter of the root. Remembering this will help you spell these words correctly.

➤ Fill in the blanks with one of the following combinations. Then write the whole word.

| occ | off | opp | diff | **Copy** |

1. Once in a while __ __ __a sion al ly _____

2. A person who lives in a place __ __ __u pant _____

3. Hard to do __ __ __ __i cult _____

4. To govern or rule harshly __ __ __ress _____

5. Not alike __ __ __ __er ent _____

6. As different as can be __ __ __o site _____

7. A happening; an event __ __ __ur rence _____

8. Beyond the bounds of

   ordinary knowledge;

   mysterious __ __ __ult _____

9. To present; to give something __ __ __er _____

10. Unpleasant; disagreeable __ __ __en sive _____

➤ Find and circle all of the words above in the puzzle below. The words can be found in a straight line across or up and down.

```
A O G S L D H O V A Z R K
O C C A S I O N A L L Y O
P C J O F F E N S I V E P
P U D I F F E R E N T I P
R R Y Q H I B I Q B X P O
E R J O C C U P A N T G S
S E O C C U L T C K W F I
S N D L E L E R W V O D T
M C S U N T C O F F E R E
B E F N T C X D U P T M A
```

Review

Changing the prefix to match the first letter of the root results in a double c_____.

➡ Your teacher will dictate some words. Sound out each word as you write the missing syllable(s). Then write the whole word, saying it aloud as you spell it.

Copy

1. _____ po   site   _____

2. _____ fer _____   _____

3. _____ vi   ous   _____

4. _____ turb _____   _____

5. _____ _____ cul _____   _____

6. dis _____   _____

7. _____ _____ bey   _____

8. _____ fer _____   _____

9. _____ gest _____   _____

10. _____ struc _____   _____

11. _____ miss _____   _____

12. _____ fen _____   _____

13. _____ il _____ _____   _____

14. _____ _____ si _____   _____

15. _____ cu _____ _____   _____

16. _____ cur _____   _____

Review

Match the rule with the word that is an example of that rule.

disability   Accent the syllable just before -*tion* or -*sion*.

occurrence   Accent the syllable just before -*ity*.

occasionally   Accent the root in most words with a prefix, root, and suffix.

★ The accent is usually on the first syllable of two- or three-syllable words. If accenting the first syllable does not make a recognizable word, accent the second syllable.

➡ Identify the accented syllables. Then copy each word by syllables under the correct heading. Write the accented syllables in the boxes.

offer	obtain	obstacle	discover	difference
disturb		disaster		occupant

Accent the First Syllable **Accent the Second Syllable**

objection	occupation	disability	occasionally	digestion
opportunity	diversion	discrimination	disposition	occasional

Accent the syllable before -*ity, -tion,* or -*sion*.

Separate and write the prefix (or assimilated prefix), root, and suffix in each of the following words. Then pronounce the words. Some words have more than one prefix or suffix.★

	Prefix	Root	Suffix	Double Letter?
occurrence	_____	_____	_____	_____
obnoxious	_____	_____	_____	_____
objection	_____	_____	_____	_____
dislocate	_____	_____	_____	_____
offensive	_____	_____	_____	_____
offering	_____	_____	_____	_____
opponent	_____	_____	_____	_____
different	_____	_____	_____	_____
diversion	_____	_____	_____	_____
digestion	_____	_____	_____	_____
digestive	_____	_____	_____	_____
disturbance	_____	_____	_____	_____
disadvantage	____ ____	_____	_____	_____
occupant	_____	_____	_____	_____
oppression	_____	_____	_____	_____
disgraceful	_____	_____	_____	_____
objectionable	_____	_____	____ ____	_____
occasional	_____	_____	____ ____	_____
occupation	_____	_____	____ ____	_____

★In some words a consonant could be placed either at the end of the root or at the beginning of the suffix. As long as you can read and spell the word, it doesn't matter which way you divide it.

➡ Many List 42 words are hard to spell because the first syllable has a schwa sound. To spell these words correctly, write the prefix (or the assimilated prefix) in full and the root in full. Remember the double consonant in many of these words.

It sounds like . . .	**but is spelled . . .**
ə pose	_____
ə cur	_____
ə press	_____
ə fend	_____
ə po nent	_____
ə cult	_____
ə fen sive	_____
ə cur rence	_____
də lute	_____
də sease	_____
də min ish	_____
də ver sion	_____
də men sion	_____
də vulge	_____

➡ Proofread this story and correct it as shown.

opponents

My ~~opponents~~ in the game had a səcessful əfensive strategy that they would not dəvulge. First, they created a dəversion to split my team in two. Then they əbscured our view. I əbjected to their tactics, but the əficial s əported them. It had never əcurred to me that my team might lose.

Your teacher will dictate some practical spelling words. Say the words aloud as you write them under the correct heading.

ob–

_____

_____

_____

oc–

_____

_____

_____

op–

_____

_____

of–

_____

dis–

_____

_____

_____

_____

_____

dif–

_____

_____

di–

_____

_____

Proofing Practice

Two common List 42 words are misspelled in each of the sentences below. Correct them as shown.

1. Is it acceptable for children to ~~disobay~~ *disobey* their parents when they disegree with them?

2. The intern found it dificult to diagnose the patient's disseez.

3. Does your oponant have an objecktion to your stand on the issue?

4. The team that played oposit us had uniforms of a diferant color.

5. Did the chemist ever diskover who disterbed the experiment?

Review

A _____ _____ is a group of words that have a common part.

➤ Complete each sentence below by using the word in the left-hand column or a member of its word family. Add one or both of the suffixes to make members of the word family. You may need to drop a letter from the root before adding the suffix(es).

object

-tion

-able

1. Do you _____ to going?

2. What is your _____ to going?

3. I don't see why you find it _____.

occasion

-ly

-al

4. It was a happy _____ when the football team won.

5. Unfortunately, the team won only _____.

6. However, an _____ win was better than none at all.

differ

-ent

-ence

7. John and Jack _____ in looks even though they are twins.

8. Their personalities are very _____.

9. One big _____ is that Jack is much taller.

dispose

-al

10. We _____ of our trash in the garbage _____.

disinfect

-ant

11. The orderly used a _____ to _____ the hospital room.

difficult

-y

12. Some people have a great deal of _____ learning how to spell.

13. Does *Megawords* make spelling less _____ for you?

oppress

-sion

-ive

14. The peasants may rebel if the king continues to _____ them.

15. Such _____ of the people by unjust rulers has caused war in the past.

16. _____ measures were taken to crush the rebellion.

➡ Use the words below to complete the puzzle.

dilute	divulge	dilate	diffuse	diminish
dislocate	obnoxious	diverge	disaster	distinguished
discontented		oppression		occult

Across

2. Great; worthy of being remembered

4. Spread out; scattered

6. Secret; hidden; mysterious

7. To go in different directions

8. Dissatisfied; unhappy

9. To make wider or larger

10. Offensive; disagreeable; objectionable

Down

1. To make smaller in size or importance

2. To weaken or thin by adding water

3. A terrible event; a great misfortune

5. To put out of joint

6. Cruel or unjust use of power

7. To make known; to tell

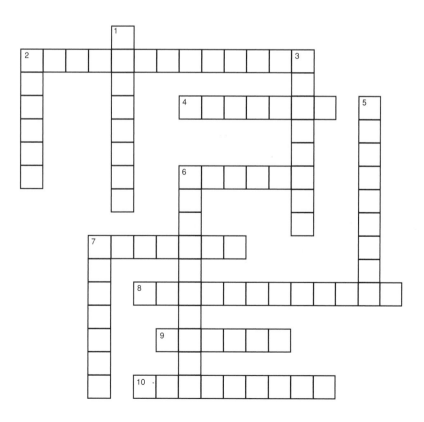

➡ Read the following sentences and circle all the List 42 words that you can find.

1. That comedian is offensive; I disapprove of his objectionable and obnoxious jokes.

2. After the doctor dilated her pupil, an eye disease was discovered.

3. Two-year-olds are occasionally obstinate and may disagree at every opportunity.

4. The mayor's opponent observed the police as they arrested the offenders.

5. I was dismissed from my filing job and offered a different job at the waste distribution center.

6. The leader of the occult sect would not divulge who wore the disguises during the ceremony even when ordered to disclose it.

7. A subcontractor offered me an opportunity to buy the items on display at a discount.

8. During the discussion, Sheila opposed any oppression of or discrimination against disadvantaged or disabled people.

9. The disturbance was obviously staged as a diversion so that the prisoners could escape.

➡ Take out a piece of blank paper. Your teacher will dictate three of the sentences above for you to write.

➡ Now select ten words from List 42 and create a short story or a descriptive paragraph that uses those words. Be creative and avoid repetition!

Reading Accuracy: Demonstrate your accuracy in reading and spelling List 42 words. Your teacher will select ten words to read and ten practical spelling words for you to spell. Record your scores on the Accuracy Checklist. Work toward 90–100 percent accuracy.

Reading Proficiency: Now build up your reading fluency with List 42 words. Decide on your rate goal with your teacher. Record your progress on the Proficiency Graph.

My goal for reading List 42 is _____ words per minute with two or fewer errors.

ex-	ef- (f)	e- (d, l, m, n, v)	syn-	sym- (b, p, m)	sys- (s) syl- (l)
* example	* effect	* editor	* syndrome	* symbol	* syllable
* excellent	* effective	* elect	* synonym	* sympathize	* system
* excitement	* efficient	* election	synagogue	* sympathy	* systematic
* executive	* effort	* elevator	synapse	* symptom	syllabic
* exercise	effectual	* emergency	synchronize	symbiosis	syllabication
* expensive	efferent	* evidence	synchronous	symbiotic	syllogism
* experience	effervesce	edit	synod	symbolism	systaltic
* explosion	efficiency	educate	synonymous	symbolize	systematize
exact	effigy	education	synopsis	symmetrical	systemic
exaggerate	effortless	elevate	syntax	symmetry	
exasperate	effrontery	eliminate	synthesis	sympathetic	
excavate	effusive	elimination	synthesize	symphonic	
exceedingly		emancipate	synthetic	symphony	
exception		emerge		symposium	
excessive		emergence		symptomatic	
excursion		emigrate			
exhaust		emission			
exhaustion		emit			
exhibit		enormous			
existence		enumerate			
expectation		evaporate			
expedition		evaporation			
extension					

*Practical spelling words. The teacher and student should decide together how many of these words the student will be responsible for spelling.

Review

Assimilated _____ are prefixes in which the final letter changes to match or better fit with the first letter of the root that follows it.

★ The prefix *ex-* means "out of," "from," or "former," as in *exception*.

ex- changes to: *ef-* before *f*, as in effort

e- before *l, m, n, d,* or *v*, as in *elect, emergency, enormous, edit,* and *evaporate*

ex- is unchanged before other letters, as in *explain* and *excitement*.

➡ Circle and pronounce the prefix *ex-* or its assimilated prefix in each of the following words. Then underline the letter that follows each prefix.

extreme	effective	edit	evaporate	excitement
educate	exhibit	effort	elect	election
exercise	excellent	emigrate	evidence	excavate
enumerate	enormous	efficient	example	expensive

★ The prefix *syn-* means "with," "along with," "together," or "at the same time," as in *sympathize*.

syn- changes to: *sym-* before *b, p,* and *m,* as in *symbol, sympathy,* and *symmetric*

sys- before *t* (sometimes), as in *system*

syl- before *l,* as in *syllable*

syn- is unchanged before other letters, as in *synagogue, syntax,* and *synonymous*.

➡ Circle and pronounce the prefix *syn-* or its assimilated prefix in each of the following words. Then underline the letter that follows each prefix.

syndrome	symmetry	systematic	syllable	synthetic
synagogue	syllabication	synchronous	systaltic	synonym
syntax	symbiotic	symphony	symbol	sympathy

Review

Give an example for each rule.

ex- changes to *ef-* before *f*, as in _____ .

syn- changes to *sym-* before *b, p,* and *m,* as in _____ .

syn- changes to *syl-* before *l,* as in _____ .

➤ Circle the prefix or assimilated prefix in these words. Underline the first letter of the root. Write the prefix and first letter of the root as shown. Then complete the rule.

(ex)treme   _ex_ + _t_   ex- doesn't _____ in front of many letters.

exercise   _____ + _____

existence   _____ + _____

effective   _____ + _____   ex- changes to _____ in front of _____.

effort   _____ + _____

election   _____ + _____   ex- changes to _____ in front of _____,

educate   _____ + _____   _____, _____, and _____.

emergency   _____ + _____

evidence   _____ + _____

syndrome   _____ + _____   syn- doesn't _____ in front of many

synapse   _____ + _____   letters.

synthesize   _____ + _____

symbol   _____ + _____   syn- changes to _____ in front of _____,

sympathy   _____ + _____   _____, and _____.

symmetry   _____ + _____

system   _____ + _____   syn- changes to _____ in front of _____,

systematic   _____ + _____   sometimes.

syllogism   _____ + _____   syn- changes to _____ in front of _____.

➤ Your teacher will dictate some words that contain the prefixes *syn*- and *ex*-. Write the prefix or assimilated prefix and the first letter of the root as shown.

1. _e_ / _l_   3. _____ / _____   5. _____ / _____   7. _____ / _____

2. _____ / _____   4. _____ / _____   6. _____ / _____   8. _____ / _____

➡ Pronounce and combine the syllables. Then cover the divided word and practice reading the whole word. Study the accent pattern and draw a box around the accented syllable.

__ ´ __

sym bol	symbol
sys tem	system
ed it	edit

__ __ ´

ex act	exact
e lect	elect
ef fect	effect

__ ´ __ __

ed it or	editor
el e vate	elevate
syl la ble	syllable
ex cel lent	excellent
sym pa thy	sympathy

__ __ ´ __

e nor mous	enormous
syn thet ic	synthetic
syl lab ic	syllabic
ex cite ment	excitement
sym phon ic	symphonic

__ ´ __ __ __

ex cel len cy	excellency

__ __ ´ __ __

e mer gen cy	emergency
e lim i nate	eliminate
syn on y mous	synonymous
e nor mi ty	enormity

__ __ __ ´ __

ex pec ta tion	expectation
sym pa thet ic	sympathetic

__ __ __ __ ´ __

e vap or a tion	evaporation
syl lab i ca tion	syllabication
e lim i na tion	elimination

__ __ __ ´ __ __

in ef fec tu al	ineffectual

➡️ Match the prefixes with the roots to make words. Then say each word aloud as you write it.

ex	fect	*extreme*	e	tax	_____
sym	lect	_____	ef	tom	_____
ef	treme	_____	syn	merge	_____
sys	bol	_____	symp	it	_____
e	tem	_____	ed	fort	_____

➡️ Unscramble these multisyllabic words. If you circle the prefix and underline the suffix or a familiar ending, you will know which syllables begin and end the word.

sive pen ex   _____

fi ef cient   _____

i ev dence   _____

mous nor e   _____

ble la syl   _____

ic thet syn   _____

tion e lec   _____

pa sym ic thet   _____

vap or e ate   _____

ta ex pec tion   _____

lim e i nate   _____

u tive ex ec   _____

cess ex ive ly   _____

sys te ic mat   _____

mat symp ic to   _____

pe tion di ex   _____

ex per as ate   _____

Review

The prefix *ex-* changes to _____ before *f* and to _____ before *l, m, n, d,* and *v.*

The prefix *syn-* changes to _____ before *b, p,* and *m,* to _____ before *t* (sometimes),

and to _____ before *l.*

➤ Circle the first letter of the syllable next to the blank, and write the prefix *ex-* or *syn-* or one of their assimilated prefixes in the blank. Use the review as a key. Then pronounce the word as you write it.

Add *ex-, ef-,* or *e-*	**Copy**	**ABC Order**
_____ fort	_____	_____
_____ treme	_____	_____
_____ lect	_____	_____
_____ vap o rate	_____	_____
_____ is tence	_____	_____
_____ fect	_____	_____
_____ mer gen cy	_____	_____
_____ cel lent	_____	_____

Add *syn-, sym-, sys-,* or *syl-*	**Copy**	**ABC Order**
_____ pa thy	_____	_____
_____ la ble	_____	_____
_____ o nym	_____	_____
_____ pho ny	_____	_____
_____ bol	_____	_____
_____ met ri cal	_____	_____
_____ thet ic	_____	_____
_____ tem	_____	_____

➤ Now go back and write the words in alphabetical order.

➤ Your teacher will dictate some words. Sound out each word as you write the missing syllable(s). Then write the whole word, saying it aloud as you spell it.

Copy

1. _____ cite _____   _____

2. _____ pen _____   _____

3. _____ tem   _____

4. _____ la   ble   _____

5. _____ fort   _____

6. _____ thet _____   _____

7. _____ lec _____   _____

8. _____ mer _____ cy   _____

9. ed _____   _____

10. _____ lim i _____   _____

11. ev _____ _____   _____

12. _____ am _____   _____

13. _____ bol _____   _____

14. _____ pect   _____

15. _____ _____ thy   _____

➤ Find and circle all of the words above in the puzzle below. The words can be found in a straight line across or up and down.

```
A E X E D I T S Y M B O L I C Y S
E X P E N S S Y L L A B L E A S Y
V A E X P E N S I V E E L E C K N
I M S Y N T H T E F F O R T N A T
D P E X A M P E L I M I N A T E H
E L E M E R E M S Y M P A T H Y E
N E X P E C T E X C I T E M E N T
C S Y L E M E R G E N C Y E F F I
E X A E L E C T I O N S Y M P A C
```

Separate and write the prefix (or assimilated prefix), root, and suffix in each of the following words. Then pronounce the words. Some words have more than one suffix.★

	Prefix	Root	Suffix	Double Letter?
extension	_____	_____	_____	_____
effective	_____	_____	_____	_____
exception	_____	_____	_____	_____
synthetic	_____	_____	_____	_____
systemic	_____	_____	_____	_____
exhaustion	_____	_____	_____	_____
existence	_____	_____	_____	_____
synthesize	_____	_____	_____	_____
emergence	_____	_____	_____	_____
syllabic	_____	_____	_____	_____
enormous	_____	_____	_____	_____
expensive	_____	_____	_____	_____
excitement	_____	_____	_____	_____
efficient	_____	_____	_____	_____
symbolize	_____	_____	_____	_____
sympathize	_____	_____	_____	_____
effortlessly	_____	_____	____ ____	_____
expectation	_____	_____	____ ____	_____
symphony	_____	_____	_____	_____
effectual	_____	_____	____ ____	_____

*In some words a consonant could be placed either at the end of the root or at the beginning of the suffix. As long as you can read and spell the word, it doesn't matter which way you divide it.

Identify the accented syllables. Then copy each word by syllables. Write the accented syllables in the boxes.

The accent is usually on the first syllable in two- or three-syllable words.

system

evidence

editor

Accent the root in words composed of a prefix and root or a prefix, root, and suffix.

elect

effective

expensive

Accent the syllable before *-tion* or *-sion*.

emission

extension

emigration

expectation

evaporation

syllabication

Your teacher will dictate some practical spelling words. Say the words aloud as you write them under the correct heading.

ex-

_____

_____

_____

_____

_____

ef-

_____

_____

_____

e-

_____

_____

_____

syn-

_____

_____

sys-

_____

_____

syl-

_____

sym-

_____

_____

_____

Proofing Practice

Two common List 43 words are misspelled in each of the sentences below. Correct them as shown.

exercise
1. You will get more ~~excercize~~ if you do not take the elavator.

2. The nurse provided simpethy as the patient was wheeled into the emerjency room.

3. Senator Carp exerted much efort to win this elekshun.

4. Exibit A, the suspect's gun, was submitted as evidance in the murder trial.

5. A good edjukashun will have a lasting efect on your life.

Review

A _____ _____ is a group of words that have a common part.

➡ Complete each sentence below by using the word in the left-hand column or a member of its word family. Add one or more of the suffixes to make members of the word family. You may need to add, drop, or change letters in the word before adding the suffix(es).

sympathy	1. After she fell, the child ran to her father for some _____.
-ize	2. The nurse's aide was very _____; part of his job was
-ic	to _____ with the hospital patients.
symbol	3. Ben Franklin wanted the wild turkey to be the _____
-ic	of our country, but the bald eagle was chosen instead.
-ism	4. In cartoons, a light bulb often _____ someone's
-izes	getting an idea.
	5. There is often much _____ in poetry.
	6. The stars and stripes on the American flag are _____;
	the stars represent the 50 states and the stripes represent the 13 colonies.
efficient	7. My aunt is a very _____ manager.
-cy	8. Her _____ is especially valued during the holiday rush.
elevate	9. Denver is called the "Mile High City" because its _____ is
-tion	one mile.
-or	10. Use the stairs instead of taking the _____ if you are
-ed	going up or down only one or two flights.
	11. Part of the transit system in Chicago is _____ and
	called the "El."
exhaust	12. I was _____ after the soccer game. In fact, my
-tion	_____ had never been greater.
-ed	13. Cars emit _____ that is harmful to the environment.

Use the words below to complete the puzzle.

syllable   emerge   syndrome   exercise   symmetry

emit   synagogue   exhibit   system   eliminate

synonym   synthetic   evaporate   symbiotic   efficient

evidence

Across

1. A group of symptoms that have to do with a disease or medical condition
5. To display; something shown to the public
6. To disappear; to change into vapor
7. A word that means the same as another word
9. One or more letters in a word pronounced as a unit
11. Regular proportions; harmony; similar design on both sides of something
13. To exert the body; to use
14. Proof; testimony
15. Able to do things without waste

Down

1. A Jewish house of worship
2. To give off; to discharge
3. To get rid of; to exclude
4. Made artificially
8. Pertaining to dissimilar organisms living together in a mutually beneficial relationship
10. To come into view
12. A method or plan for doing things

➡ Read the following sentences and circle all the List 43 words that you can find.

1. My exceptionally efficient secretary systematized my files and eliminated duplication.

2. If your temperature remains elevated over 102°, go to the emergency room.

3. The editor has evidence that the executive tried to fix the election.

4. The climber's exhaustion after the expedition to Mount McKinley was due to the exceedingly cold temperatures and the high elevation.

5. Has learning about syllables and syllabication in *Megawords* helped your reading?

6. An excellent way to promote exercise would be to eliminate elevators.

7. Are her fever and rash symptoms of some syndrome or of a systemic disease?

8. My math teacher has a systematic way of teaching us symbols for symmetry and other concepts.

9. An exceedingly large crowd attended the excellent exhibit of Egyptian art.

10. At the symposium, the synagogue next to Symphony Hall was designated a landmark.

➡ Take out a piece of blank paper. Your teacher will dictate three of the sentences above for you to write.

➡ Now select ten words from List 43 and create a short story or a descriptive paragraph that uses those words. Be creative and avoid repetition!

Reading Accuracy: Demonstrate your accuracy in reading and spelling List 43 words. Your teacher will select ten words to read and ten practical spelling words for you to spell. Record your scores on the Accuracy Checklist. Work toward 90–100 percent accuracy.

Reading Proficiency: Now build up your reading fluency with List 43 words. Decide on your rate goal with your teacher. Record your progress on the Proficiency Graph.

My goal for reading List 43 is _____ words per minute with two or fewer errors.

LIST 44: ASSIMILATED PREFIX *in-*

in- (in)	*in-* (not)	*im-* (in)	*im-* (not)	*il-* (in)	*il-* (not)
* included	* incomplete	* important	* immediate	* illustrate	* illegal
* increase	* indefinite	* improvement	* immediately	illuminate	illegible
* indicate	* individual	imbed	* impatient	illumination	illegitimate
* investment	inability	imbibe	* impolite	illusion	illicit
incidence	inaccessible	immerse	* impossible	illustrative	illiterate
incite	inaccurate	immigrant	imbecile	illustrious	
incubate	inactive	immigrate	immature		
inflammable	incapable	impeach	immobile	*ir-* (in)	*ir-* (not)
influential	incessant	impending	immortal		
inhale	incoherent	imply	immune	irrigate	* irregular
insert	incompetent	import	immunity	irrigation	irrational
insidious	inconceivable	impress	impartial		irrelevant
insistent	inconvenient	imprison	impersonal		irreparable
intense	incredible	impulse	impurity		irresistible
intention	incurable	impulsive			irresponsible
	indecent				irreverent
	indigestion				
	indiscreet				
	indisposed				
	inefficient				
	inexcusable				
	inorganic				
	invalid (adj.)				

*Practical spelling words. The teacher and student should decide together how many of these words the student will be responsible for spelling.

Review

_____ _____ are prefixes in which the

final letter changes to match or better fit with the first letter of the root that follows it.

★ The prefix *in-* has two meanings:

1. "not" or "opposite of," as in *incomplete*

2. "in" or "into," as in *insert*

in- changes to: *im-* before *m, p,* and *b,* as in *immense, imperfect,* and *imbecile*

        il- before *l,* as in *illegal*

        ir- before *r,* as in *irregular*

in- is unchanged before most letters, as in *intense, inhale,* and *inactive.*

➡ Circle and pronounce the prefix *in-* or its assimilated prefix in each of the following words. Then underline the letter that follows each prefix.

impolite	illusion	irregular	indigestion	impossible
improve	individual	immediate	illicit	illegal
increase	indicate	included	irrigate	influential
irresistible		imply		illegible

➡ Find and circle the eighteen words above in the puzzle below. The words can be found in a straight line across or up and down. Write the leftover letters in the blanks below.

```
I R R E S I S T I B L E T I N D I V I D U A L I
M H Y O I M P O L I T E I M P O S S I B L E W L
P N I R R E G U L A R I M P I R R I G A T E P L
R O R I N F L U E N T I A L T I N C L U D E D I
O A N C I L L E G I B L E Y I N D I C A T E E C
V K I M M E D I A T E N I N D I G E S T I O N I
E O W P O P I L L U S I O N E I N C R E A S E T
```

___ ___   ___ ___ ___   ___ ___ ___ ___ ___ ___ ___ ___ ___   ___ ___ ___ ___

                 ___ ___ ___ ___ ___

➤ Circle the prefix or assimilated prefix in these words. Underline the first letter of the root. Write the prefix and first letter of the root as shown. Then complete the rule.

(in)accurate ___in___ + ___a___   *in-* doesn't change in front of most _____.

incapable _____ + _____

indecent _____ + _____

inefficient _____ + _____

influential _____ + _____

inhale _____ + _____

intense _____ + _____

inorganic _____ + _____

improve _____ + _____   *in-* changes to _____ in front of _____,

important _____ + _____   _____, and _____.

immense _____ + _____

immigrant _____ + _____

imbed _____ + _____

imbecile _____ + _____

illuminate _____ + _____   *in-* changes to _____ in front of _____.

illegal _____ + _____

irrational _____ + _____   *in-* changes to _____ in front of _____.

irregular _____ + _____

➤ Your teacher will dictate some words that contain the prefix *in-*. Write the prefix or assimilated prefix and the first letter of the root as shown.

1. __in__/__c__   3. _____/____   5. _____/____   7. _____/____

2. _____/____   4. _____/____   6. _____/____   8. _____/____

➤ Pronounce and combine the syllables. Then cover the divided word and practice reading the whole word. Study the accent pattern and draw a box around the accented syllable. Remember that the vowel in unaccented syllables frequently has the schwa sound.

__ ´__

im	port	import
im	pulse	impulse
im	passe	impasse
im	pact	impact

__ __ ´

im	prove	improve
im	mense	immense
in	cite	incite
im	pose	impose

__ ´__ __

im	mi	grant	immigrant
ir	ri	gate	irrigate
im	be	cile	imbecile
in	di	cate	indicate

__ __ ´__

il	lu	sion	illusion
im	per	fect	imperfect
im	por	tant	important
il	le	gal	illegal

__ __ __ ´__

in	di	ges	tion	indigestion
im	per	fec	tion	imperfection
in	or	gan	ic	inorganic
il	lus	tra	tion	illustration

__ __ ´__ __

ir	rel	e	vant	irrelevant
in	ca	pa	ble	incapable
in	com	pe	tent	incompetent
ir	reg	u	lar	irregular

__ __ __ ´__ __

ir	re	sis	ti	ble	irresistible
in	a	bil	i	ty	inability
in	ac	ces	si	ble	inaccessible
in	ex	cu	sa	ble	inexcusable
il	le	git	i	mate	illegitimate

__ __ ´__ __ __

im	me	di	ate	ly	immediately

__ __ __ __ ´__ __

im	pos	si	bil	i	ty	impossibility

➤ Unscramble these multisyllabic words. If you circle the prefix and underline the suffix or a familiar ending, you will know which syllables begin and end the word.

di   in   cate   _____

in   ant   cess   _____

par   tial   im   _____

tient   im   pa   _____

sion   lu   il   _____

cent   de   in   _____

vest   ment   in   _____

al   son   per   im   _____

her   in   co   ent   _____

ous   lus   il   tri   _____

ble   im   poss   i   _____

tion   in   di   ges   _____

u   ir   reg   lar   _____

ate   me   im   di   _____

di   im   me   ate   ly   _____

re   ir   sist   ble   i   _____

ble   re   ir   si   spon   _____

i   si   im   bil   ty   pos   _____

Review

Give an example for each rule.

in- changes to *il-* before *l*, as in _____.

in- changes to *ir-* before *r*, as in _____.

in- changes to *im-* before *p*, as in _____.

Review

The prefix *in-* changes to _____ before *m*, *b*, and *p*, to _____ before *l*, and to _____ before *r*.

➡ Circle the first letter of the syllable next to the blank, and write the prefix *in-* or one of its assimilated prefixes in the blank. Use the review as a key. Then pronounce the word as you write it.

Add *in-* or *ir-*	Copy	**Add *im-* or *il-***	Copy
_____ reg u lar	_____	_____ port	_____
_____ com plete	_____	_____ lu sion	_____
_____ flu en tial	_____	_____ me di ate ly	_____
_____ ri gate	_____	_____ leg i ble	_____
_____ at ten tion	_____	_____ mi grant	_____
_____ di ges tion	_____	_____ le gal	_____
_____ re spon si ble	_____	_____ por tant	_____

★ Some List 44 words have double consonants because the final letter of the prefix changes to match the first letter of the root. Remembering this will help you spell these words correctly.

➡ Fill in the blanks with one of the following combinations. Then write the whole word.

imm	ill	irr	Copy

1. Right away	__ __ __ e di ate ly	_____
2. Not mature	__ __ __a ture	_____
3. Not legal	__ __ __e gal	_____
4. Move into a foreign country	__ __ __i grate	_____
5. Huge	__ __ __ense	_____
6. Not regular	__ __ __eg u lar	_____
7. Decorate with pictures	__ __ __us trate	_____

➡ Your teacher will dictate some words. Sound out each word as you write the missing syllable(s). Then write the whole word, saying it aloud as you spell it.

Copy

1. _____ _____ lite   _____

2. _____ _____ di   ate _____   _____

3. _____ prove _____   _____

4. _____ _____ si _____   _____

5. _____ _____ ed   _____

6. _____ ac _____   _____

7. _____ vest _____   _____

8. _____ le _____   _____

9. _____ mi _____   _____

10. _____ lus tri _____   _____

11. _____ ri _____ _____   _____

12. _____ _____ sion   _____

13. _____ por _____   _____

14. in _____ en _____   _____

15. ir_____ u _____   _____

Review

The prefix *in-* changes to _____ before *r*, to _____ before *l*, and to _____ before *m, p,* and *b*.

Review

Match the rule with the word that is an example of that rule.

inability	Accent the syllable just before *-tion* or *-sion*.
irrigation	Accent the syllable just before *-ity*.
impossible	Accent the root in most words with a prefix, root, and suffix.
inactive	*-able* and *-ible* are unaccented endings.

➡ Identify the accented syllables. Then copy each word by syllables under the correct heading. Write the accented syllables in the boxes. Mark the accented vowels.

intense	important	irresistible	invest	immense
inconceivable	inability	inactive	impressionable	impurity
improvement	incurable	intensity	impossible	incapable
indigestion	influential	illumination	irresponsible	irrigation

Accent the Second Syllable

Accent the Second Syllable

Accent the Third Syllable

Accent the Third Syllable

Accent the Fourth Syllable

➤ Separate and write the prefix (or assimilated prefix), root, and suffix in each of the following words. Then pronounce the words. Some words have more than one prefix, root, or suffix.★

	Prefix	**Root**	**Suffix**
impossible	_____	_____	_____
immortal	_____	_____	_____
important	_____	_____	_____
impulsive	_____	_____	_____
inflammable	_____	_____	_____
impartial	_____	_____	_____
impending	_____	_____	_____
intensity	_____	_____	_____
indigestion	_____	_____	_____
inconvenient	_____	_____	_____
incompetent	_____	_____	_____
irresistible	____ ____	_____	_____
irresponsible	____ ____	_____	_____
inactive	_____	_____	_____
improvement	_____	_____	_____
incidental	_____	_____	_____
immediately	_____	____ ____	____ ____

➤ Choose one of the words above and use it in a sentence.

_____

★In some words a consonant could be placed at the end of the root or at the beginning of the suffix. As long as you can read and spell the word, it doesn't matter which way you divide it.

Your teacher will dictate some practical spelling words. Say the words aloud as you write them under the correct heading.

im–	*in–*	*il–*
_____	_____	_____
_____	_____	_____
_____	_____	
_____	_____	
_____	_____	
_____		
_____	*ir–*	
_____	_____	

Proofing Practice

Two common List 44 words are misspelled in each of the sentences below. Correct them as shown.

1. After Roger took the medicine, we noted an ~~immedeate~~ *immediate* improvment in his health.

2. Mr. Haskins inclooded the conductor of the symphony orchestra on his list of importent guests.

3. My plans for next year are indefanite and incommplete.

4. The waitress finds impashent diners who are also impolight and offensive.

5. Jason illustraited his incredable story with an impressive drawing.

6. Please inducate the type of imvestments you are interested in.

7. Have the newspapers reported an iccrease in the use of ilegal drugs recently?

Choose two of the words your teacher dictated and use them in sentences.

_____

_____

A _____ _____ is a group of words that have a common part.

➡ Complete each sentence below by using the word in the left-hand column or a member of its word family. Add one or more of the suffixes to make members of the word family. You may need to drop a letter from the word before adding the suffix(es).

impress

-ive

-ion

-ed

-able

1. Jordan was very _____ by the hero's courage.

2. Since children are _____ the teacher would only read stories with positive messages to her students.

3. That was an _____ speech the president gave; it made a strong _____ on the audience.

improve

-ment

-ed

4. Gretchen's handwriting has _____ immensely this year.

5. Her teacher complimented her on her _____.

6. I need to work hard to _____ my handwriting.

immigrate

-tion

-ant

-ed

7. Many Italians _____ to America in 1918.

8. Julio is an _____ from Chile.

9. Visitors to the United States must pass through _____ and customs before they are permitted to enter the country.

10. Quotas specify how many people from a given country can _____ to the United States each year.

impulse

-ive

11. The _____ child acted on _____ rather than waiting to think things through.

immense

-ity

12. The Grand Canyon is _____

13. Many people are awed by its _____.

Complete each sentence with the word from below that can be used in place of the underlined word(s). Use a dictionary to look up the meaning of unfamiliar words. Write the words in the puzzle.

irresistible	incredible	incoherent	imply	illusion
influential	irrational	immortal	illegal	incessant
immigrants	incited	immobile	impasse	impeach

Across

4. Her leg was put in a cast to make sure that it was <u>unable to move.</u>
5. I find peppermint candy <u>hard to resist</u>.
7. I often wish I could be <u>alive forever and never die</u>.
8. In many states it is <u>not legal</u> to set off firecrackers.
9. It seems <u>beyond belief</u> that Marco Polo could have traveled so far.
10. The angry man ranted and raved in an <u>inconsistent and confused</u> way.
11. The judge was very <u>powerful and exerted a strong influence</u>.
12. Since neither side would give in, the teams have reached a(n) <u>deadlock.</u>
13. The three-year-old's chattering seemed to be <u>continuous</u>.

Down

1. Do you mean to <u>suggest</u> that I am too young to drive?
2. It is <u>not rational</u> to be afraid of the number 13.
3. A mirage is an <u>optical appearance that is not real</u>.
4. The <u>new settlers</u> came from Europe to New York City.
6. The rebel leader <u>urged</u> on the crowd to riot.
8. The senate voted to <u>accuse</u> the senator who was caught taking bribes.

➡ Read the following sentences and circle all the List 44 words that you can find.

1. Irrigation was impossible during the drought.

2. I know it is inconvenient and I realize you are impatient, but there will be an indefinite wait until the part for your appliance arrives.

3. Robin was an impulsive child whose schoolwork was often illegible and incomplete.

4. The politician promised immediate improvements in immigration policies for individuals.

5. This interesting and influential writer was once illiterate.

6. Inefficient, incompetent, and incapable workers do not impress the boss.

7. We are all impressed by the improvement physical therapy has made on Mindy's immobile leg.

8. The senator was caused irreparable harm by inaccurate and irrelevant reporting.

9. The investment banker was indisposed owing to a bout of indigestion.

➡ Take out a piece of blank paper. Your teacher will dictate three of the sentences above for you to write.

➡ Now select ten words from List 44 and create a short story or a descriptive paragraph that uses those words. Be creative and avoid repetition!

Reading Accuracy: Demonstrate your accuracy in reading and spelling List 44 words. Your teacher will select ten words to read and ten practical spelling words for you to spell. Record your scores on the Accuracy Checklist. Work toward 90–100 percent accuracy.

Reading Proficiency: Now build up your reading fluency with List 44 words. Decide on your rate goal with your teacher. Record your progress on the Proficiency Graph.

My goal for reading List 44 is _____ words per minute with two or fewer errors.

* accurate	* conductor	* impatient	adjustment	incubate
* adjective	* connection	* impolite	affirmation	indecent
* advertise	* contribute	* increase	allowance	indigestion
* affectionate	* convenient	* objection	coerce	inorganic
* aggression	* cooperate	* occasional	coincide	irresponsible
* appliance	* coordinate	* occupation	compel	irrigate
* appreciate	* correct	* opponent	corruption	obsolete
* arrest	* corrective	* submarine	differentiate	obstacle
* assertive	* difference	* subscribe	digestive	occupy
* assistant	* difficulty	* substitute	dimension	opportunity
* assume	* disappear	* subtract	diminish	subconscious
* attendance	* educate	* suburban	disability	subsequent
* attention	* effective	* successful	discontinue	substantial
* attract	* efficient	* suggested	discriminate	success
* attractive	* election	* supply	distinguished	suffer
* collection	* elevator	* support	emergency	suffocate
* combination	* evidence	* suspect	exhibit	supplement
* command	* excitement	* suspicious	expectation	suspension
* commission	* executive	* syllable	illegible	symptom
* complain	* illegal	* sympathize	imprison	symptomatic
* complicated	* illustrate	* synonym	improvement	synagogue
* computer	* immediate	* system	incapable	synthetic

*Practical spelling words. The teacher and student should decide together how many of these words the student will be responsible for spelling.

Accented Syllable—An accented syllable is pronounced as if it were a one-syllable word with a clear vowel sound according to its syllabic type *(ac´ tive, com plete´, ser´ vant, loy´ al)*.

Unaccented Syllable—An unaccented syllable is pronounced with a schwa /ə/ or short-i /ĭ/ vowel sound regardless of its syllabic type *(rib´ bon, op´ po site, in de pen´ dent)*.

Accent Patterns—The dark lines and accent marks in this book are accent patterns (__´ __). Each line stands for one syllable. The accent mark shows which syllable is accented. Learning to place the accent on the proper syllable will help you recognize most multisyllabic words. The accent patterns below will help you determine which syllable in a word is accented.

Primary Accent—A strong stress on a syllable in a multisyllabic word.

Secondary Accent—A weaker stress on a syllable in a multisyllabic word.

General Guideline—In two- and three-syllable words, accent the first syllable. Then pronounce the first vowel as if it were a short, long, r-controlled, or double-vowel sound in a one-syllable word. If that doesn't make a recognizable word, accent the second syllable, and pronounce the second vowel according to its syllabic type.

ACCENT PATTERNS FOR TWO-SYLLABLE WORDS

1. **Accent on the first syllable (__´ __)**
   The accent is usually on the first syllable in two-syllable words *(stan´ dard, sis´ ter, dol´ lar)*.

2. **Accent on the second syllable (__ __´)**
   Two-syllable words that have a prefix in the first syllable and a root in the second syllable are usually accented on the second syllable *(ex tend´, con fuse´)*.

3. **Accent on either the first or second syllable (__´ __ or __ __´)**
   If a word can function as both noun and verb, the noun is accented on the prefix *(con´ duct)* and the verb is accented on the root *(con duct´)*.

ACCENT PATTERNS FOR THREE-SYLLABLE WORDS

1. **Accent on the first syllable (__´ __ __)**
   The accent is usually on the first syllable in three-syllable words. The unaccented middle syllable has a schwa sound *(vis´ i tor, char´ ac ter)*.

2. **Accent on the second syllable (__ __´ __)**
   The accent is usually on the second syllable (the root) in words that contain a prefix, root, and suffix *(de stroy´ er, in ven´ tor)*.

ACCENT PATTERNS FOR FOUR-SYLLABLE WORDS (__ __´ __ __)

1. The accent is usually on the second syllable in four-syllable words *(in tel´ li gence, sig nif´ i cant)*.

SPECIAL ACCENT PATTERNS FOR WORDS OF THREE OR MORE SYLLABLES

Accent patterns for words longer than two syllables are often governed by a specific ending pattern or an unaccented vowel.

1. **Accent with the ending –ic**
   Accent the syllable just before the ending -ic *(fran´ tic, e las´ tic, en er get´ ic, char ac ter is´ tic)*.

2. **Accent with the ending –ate /āt/**
   In three-syllable words, the first syllable has a primary accent and -ate has a secondary accent *(vi´ o late´)*.
   In four-syllable words, the second syllable has a primary accent and -ate has a secondary accent *(con grat´ u late´)*.

3. **Accent with schwa endings**
   Schwa endings (and schwa syllables) are never accented. The accent falls on another syllable in the word *(pleas´ ant, in´ no cent, ex ter´ nal, ap pren´ tice)*.

4. **Accent with the endings –tion, –sion, –cian**
   Accent the syllable just before the endings -tion, -sion, and -cian *(pol lu´ tion, im pres´ sion, ad min is tra´ tion, e lec tri´ cian)*.

5. **Accent with the ending –ity /ĭ tē/**
   Accent the syllable just before the ending -ity *(qual´ i ty, ac tiv´ i ty, per son al´ i ty)*.

6. **Accent in words with an unaccented middle syllable**
   Accent the syllable just before the unaccented middle syllable with i as /ə/, i as /ē/, and u as /ə/ or /ū/ *(sim´ i lar, aud´ i ence, par tic´ u lar)*.

7. **Accent in words with i as /y/**
   Accent the syllable just before the unaccented syllable with i as /ē/ *(com pan´ ion, in con ven´ ient, mem or a bil´ ia)*.

8. **Accent in words with ti or ci as /sh/**
   Accent the syllable just before a final syllable with ti or ci as /sh/ *(fi nan´ cial, pres i den´ tial)*.

ACCURACY CHECKLIST
Megawords 8, Lists 39-44

Student _____

Record accuracy score as a fraction: $\dfrac{\text{\# correct}}{\text{\# attempted}}$

List	Examples	Check Test Scores Date:		Reading			Spelling		
		Reading	Spelling						
39. Assimilated Prefix *com-*	correspond commander								
40. Assimilated Prefix *ad-*	affirmative arrival								
41. Assimilated Prefix *sub-*	supplement suggestion								
42. Assimilated Prefixes *ob-* and *dis-*	opponent difficulty								
43. Assimilated Prefixes *ex-* and *syn-*	effective symbolize								
44. Assimilated Prefix *in-*	immunity illegal								
Review: Lists 39-44									

PROFICIENCY GRAPH

Student _____   ●————● Words Read Correctly

Goal _____   x————x Errors

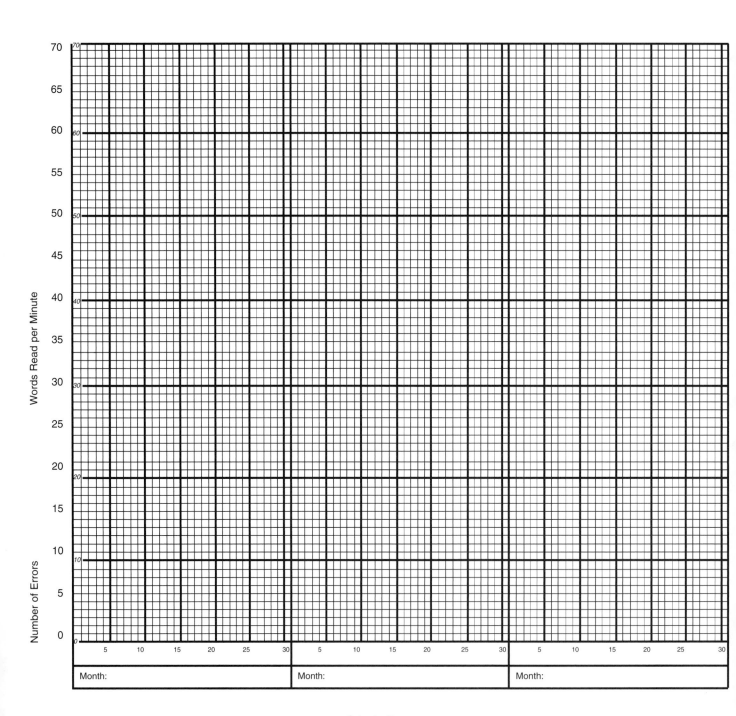

Calendar Days

Check Test: Lists 39-44

Megawords

Name _____

Date _____

39. Assimilated Prefix *com-*

consecutive

compensatory

collaborate

corruptible

coincident

correct _____

40. Assimilated Prefix *ad-*

adjudicate

appropriate

annihilate

accessories

affirmation

correct _____

41. Assimilated Prefix *sub-*

substantiate

successive

surreptitious

supplementary

susceptibility

correct _____

42. Assimilated Prefixes *ob-* and *dis-*

objectionable

occasionally

opportunity

disagreement

distinguished

correct _____

43. Assimilated Prefix *ex-* and *syn*

executive

elimination

synonym

symbolize

systematic

correct _____

44. Assimilated Prefix *in*

individual

inconvenient

illumination

irresistible

immunity

correct _____

Total Correct _____

Total Possible ___30___

EXAMINER'S RECORDING FORM – READING

Check Test: Lists 39–44

Megawords 8

39. Assimilated Prefix *com-*

consecutive

compensatory

collaborate

corruptible

coincident

correct _____

40. Assimilated Prefix *ad-*

adjudicate

appropriate

annihilate

accessories

affirmation

correct _____

41. Assimilated Prefix *sub-*

substantiate

successive

surreptitious

supplementary

susceptibility

correct _____

42. Assimilated Prefixes *ob-* and *dis-*

objectionable

occasionally

opportunity

disagreement

distinguished

correct _____

43. Assimilated Prefix *ex-* and *syn*

executive

elimination

synonym

symbolize

systematic

correct _____

44. Assimilated Prefix *in*

individual

inconvenient

illumination

irresistible

immunity

correct _____

Total Correct _____

Total Possible __30__